Journalists
Who Made History

PROFILES

Journalists
Who Made History

James Satter

The Oliver Press, Inc.
Minneapolis

The Oliver Press, Inc.
Charlotte Square
5707 West 36th Street
Minneapolis, MN 55416-2510

Library of Congress Cataloging-in-Publication Data

Satter, James, 1969-
Journalists who made history / James Satter.
p.   cm.—(Profiles)
Includes bibliographical references and index.
Summary: Profiles nine journalists whose work influenced the course
of history: Elijah Lovejoy, George Brown, Horace Greeley, William
Randolph Hearst, Ida Tarbell, Alfred Harmsworth, Edward R.
Murrow, Bob Woodward, and Carl Bernstein.
ISBN 1-881508-39-0 (lib. bdg.)
1. Journalists—Biography—Juvenile literature. [1. Journalists.]
I. Title. II. Series: Profiles (Minneapolis, Minn.)
PN4820.S38 1998
070.92'2
[B]—DC21   97-30234
                                                CIP
                                                AC

ISBN 1-881508-39-0
Printed in the United States of America

04 03 02 01 00 99 98   8 7 6 5 4 3 2 1

Contents

In the 1930s, individuals received most of their news from newspapers and magazines. The proprietors of this newsstand in St. Paul, Minnesota, were doing their part to keep Americans informed about national and world events.

Introduction

*O*ne of the telltale signs of a totalitarian society is the absence of critical debate about government leaders, political issues, and social reforms—the absence, in short, of a free press. The freedom of the press is the measure of the freedom of a society. For this reason, the men and women who have shaped the field of journalism have often also affected the course of history in their nations.

Beginning with Elijah Lovejoy, who gave his life to publish his antislavery opinions in the 1830s, *Journalists Who Made History* chronicles the lives of nine people whose careers made an impact on the world around them. Like Lovejoy, Horace Greeley helped to end slavery when, during the Civil War in the 1860s, he commanded enough public support to pressure President Abraham Lincoln to issue the Emancipation Proclamation. So confident was Greeley in his ability to change the United

States for the better that he later ran for president himself. While Greeley made a short-lived foray into politics, journalism and political leadership were inextricably linked for Canadian forefather George Brown, who in his *Toronto Globe* and in parliament was the "voice of Upper Canada."

But journalists do not need to be associated with a particular cause to influence their societies. Edward R. Murrow's trusted voice shaped public opinion as he pioneered the fields of radio and television news broadcasting from the 1930s to the 1960s. Thirty years before Murrow began broadcasting, Americans put their faith in investigative journalists such as Ida Tarbell. One of the first "muckrakers," as these journalists were called, Tarbell wrote a series of articles that brought down the monopoly of John D. Rockefeller's Standard Oil Company. Carl Bernstein and Bob Woodward carried on the muckraking tradition 70 years after Tarbell when they followed a hunch that more lurked behind a break-in at the Watergate building in Washington, D.C., than appeared at first glance. The conspiracy their investigation uncovered led to President Richard Nixon's resignation.

Other journalists were not always so committed to the truth. American newspaper publisher William Randolph Hearst and his British counterpart Alfred Harmsworth both possessed the ability to grasp exactly what their late nineteenth-century readers wanted to read—not what news was most informative or objective. By using new techniques like flashy headlines and sensational writing to manipulate the fears and desires of the

GREAT NEWSPAPERS AND EDITORS OF THE UNITED STATES.

By the end of the 1800s, William R. Hearst (second row, far right) was one of the most powerful publishers in the U.S. Here he is pictured with other major newspaper magnates, including Joseph Pulitzer (second from bottom in the middle), who taught him the business.

public for decades, the two publishers gained fantastic fortunes. They also commanded immense power over the leaders of their respective nations. Seeking greater circulation, Hearst ruthlessly stoked the American public into such a frenzy of hatred that Congress declared war against Spain in 1898. In England, Harmsworth used his newspapers to propel his government into an arms race with Germany that eventually ended in a world war. Then the publisher helped to bring down Great Britain's

9

wartime government by charging it with neglect in the conduct of that war.

There is no doubt that some journalists have abused their power to influence the public. However, restricting the freedom of the press holds more dangers. Journalists play a crucial role in keeping citizens educated and informed. United States president Thomas Jefferson once stated that it would be better to have newspapers and no government than a government and no newspapers.

Thomas Jefferson (1743-1826) founded the National Gazette *in 1791 to promote the views of what would become the Democratic Party.*

While people have always spread information by word of mouth, formal news reports date back to 59 B.C., when the Romans posted hand-written announcements called *Acta diurna*—daily events—to inform the public about current events and Senate votes. The first printed newspaper, the *Dibao*, appeared in China around A.D. 700. Reusable wood blocks were used for printing in China, Japan, and Korea in the eighth century, but mass-circulation publications were not possible until Johann Gutenberg of Germany invented a practical printing technique using movable type in the 1440s.

By the mid-1600s, as European cities began to publish newspapers regularly, the colonists who settled in North America also started their own newspapers. The debut issue of the *Boston News-Letter*, the first regularly published newspaper in North America, appeared in 1704. By 1800, nearly 2,000 budding journalists had tried printing newspapers in the colonies and early United States, often hoping to influence public opinion and political decisions. Many of these early publishers worked single-handedly as writers, editors, and printers. Their tiny papers typically were only four pages long and seldom sold more than 1,000 copies per issue. While some early papers succeeded financially, most newspapers established during the 1700s folded within two years because of high printing costs and low circulation.

Many early papers targeted specific political, social, or ethnic groups, and the modern concept of mass public appeal caught on only after 1831. In that year, Benjamin Day established the *New York Sun*, which specialized in

One of the most successful printers of the 1700s, Benjamin Franklin (1706-1790) has continued to influence readers through his famous sayings in Poor Richard's Almanack.

the crime reports, gossip, and scandals that interested the largest mass of readers. Newspapers now formed widespread public opinion instead of merely reflecting the views of small groups.

Advances in technology also revolutionized the press. By the 1850s, reporters used the electric telegraph to wire information instantly back to their offices hundreds of miles away. Telegraph wires made possible the formation of news agencies to provide what are still called wire-service reports. During the American Civil War in the 1860s, Mathew Brady pioneered the field of photojournalism as the official photographer for the Union army. Now people could see actual images from the battlefield. News came even closer to home with radio in the 1920s, television in the 1940s, and telecommunications satellites in the 1960s. Today, computers provide links to innumerable news sources by telephone lines.

As the format of news continues to change drastically, journalists will change as well. There will be new Elijah Lovejoys to defy mob violence and governmental injustice, new George Browns to use their newspapers to shape their nations, and new Ida Tarbells to protect the rights of ordinary people and small businesses from corporate giants like Standard Oil. And certainly there will be new William Randolph Hearsts prepared to set truth aside in their future battles for circulation and influence.

A man operates a sorting machine at a modern newspaper printing plant.

"I have the right freely to speak and publish my sentiments," declared Elijah Lovejoy (1802-1837) to his fellow citizens when, despite death threats, he refused to stop printing his antislavery newspaper.

1

Elijah Lovejoy
A Martyr for Free Speech

*A*s the sun beat down on July 4, 1837, the citizens of Alton, Illinois, celebrated the nation's freedom with flag waving and public speeches—everyone, that is, but Elijah Lovejoy, editor of the town's abolitionist newspaper, the *Observer*. Although Illinois was a free state, Alton lay just across the Mississippi River from the slave state of Missouri. Ever since Lovejoy began publishing articles hostile to slavery, battle lines had been drawn in the town between slavery's defenders and opponents.

Alone in his office, the editor was at it again: "What mockery is this?" he wrote in disgust. "We assemble to thank God for our own freedom . . . while our feet are on the necks of nearly three millions of our fellow men." He paused as sounds of celebration drifted in through his open window. "Even that very flag of freedom that waves over their heads is formed from materials cultivated by slaves, on a soil moistened with their blood."

The proslavery faction in Alton never forgave Lovejoy for printing this stinging rebuke. Over the next four months, they repeatedly warned the editor to censor his views; each time he steadfastly refused. The situation

After the cotton gin was invented in 1793, cotton profits soared. With this economic incentive, many southerners became intolerant of antislavery activism.

exploded in early November when an enraged mob murdered Lovejoy. But as a martyr to the antislavery message, Lovejoy would be far stronger in death than in life.

Elijah Parish Lovejoy was born in Albion, Maine, on November 9, 1802. The first of Reverend Daniel and Elizabeth Lovejoy's seven children, Elijah was an especially bright boy who could read the Bible by the time he was four years old. Through his Christian upbringing, Elijah developed firm opinions of right and wrong as well as a faith in an afterlife—convictions that help to explain his fearlessness to die for his cause.

In autumn 1823, Elijah entered Waterville College (now Colby College) in Maine, about a dozen miles from Albion. Even though he was a model student, the young man battled depression. He had yet to undergo what was called a "conversion"—an intense religious experience many Protestants believed was necessary for salvation. "Without it I am miserable indeed," he told his father.

Lovejoy graduated from Waterville in September 1826 at the head of his class. He took a teaching job in nearby China, Maine, but soon the restless Lovejoy decided to move west to the new state of Illinois. He would spread religion and culture among the settlers.

Too poor to pay for transportation, Lovejoy walked the Boston-to-New York leg of his journey. Helped by a timely loan from the president of his old college, he finally arrived in Hillsboro, Illinois, in autumn 1827, worn out from his 1,200-mile trip. Since prospects for employment seemed brighter further west in Missouri, Lovejoy again set out on foot.

When he crossed the Mississippi River to St. Louis, Missouri, the city boasted a population of over 6,000 people—a huge number for a frontier town in the late 1820s. Missouri had only a smattering of schools, so the 25-year-old decided to start his own high school, modeled on the academies he had known growing up. He would teach "good New England culture" to the westerners.

Despite his school's success, Lovejoy tired of teaching. He wanted to write and make an impact on society. In the summer of 1830, he bought into a local newspaper, the *St. Louis Times*. Closing his school, Lovejoy began editing the paper. As editor, he commissioned articles and checked them for mistakes. He also wrote columns expressing his views. Thus began a turbulent career that would end with his murder less than eight years later.

Lovejoy and his partner, T. J. Miller, lost no time taking sides in the political battles that characterized journalism in the 1830s. From his first day as an editor in a slave state, Lovejoy held views hostile to most southerners. While not bankrolled by any political party, the *Times* openly opposed President Andrew Jackson. Lovejoy labeled him a "murderer" for his brutal policy of forcibly removing the Creek and Cherokee Indians from valuable lands in the East. Western settlers and smaller southern slaveholders and farmers—groups well represented in Missouri—were President Jackson's ardent supporters.

The national politician Lovejoy favored most was Henry Clay, a powerful congressman unpopular with southern planters because of his support for a *tariff*, or tax, on foreign imports. Southerners felt that if a tariff was

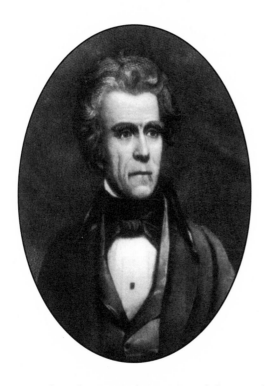

White slaveholders established new cotton plantations on the land Andrew Jackson (1767-1845) opened up by forcing the American Indians to move west.

placed on goods imported from other nations, then these countries would not purchase southern crops like tobacco, rice, and cotton.

Clay also supported the American Colonization Society, founded in 1817 for the purpose of returning freed slaves to Africa. But while Lovejoy showed interest in the colonization society, he was by no means in favor of granting slaves immediate freedom. In fact, during his early days at the paper, the *Times* regularly ran advertisements for slave sales.

Only in January 1832 did the editor seriously begin questioning the morality of slavery. That month, he attended a fiery sermon delivered by a visiting minister, David Nelson, who attacked the selling of human beings as an abomination to God. Something inside Lovejoy suddenly clicked. As he wrote to his mother shortly thereafter, he had finally received "just what I have prayed for with all my heart"—his conversion.

Overcome with a desire to spread his new faith, Lovejoy left the newspaper business. For a year, he studied to become a minister, then preached along the Eastern Seaboard for several months. But by the summer of 1833, Lovejoy had grown tired with the routine of a job that seemed too much like teaching. A new opportunity came when a group of Christian businessmen, eager to promote religion in Missouri, offered Lovejoy a position as editor of a newspaper they were starting in St. Louis.

Lovejoy returned to St. Louis on November 12, 1833. The first issue of the *St. Louis Observer* appeared 10 days later. The paper would focus on "Christian politics, the diffusion [spreading] of religious intelligence, and the salvation of souls," wrote Lovejoy. And the *Observer*, he claimed, would never "fear to speak out" about the truth.

In addition to editing the weekly paper, Lovejoy preached to religious societies as a representative of the American Home Missionary Society. Just as he minced no words in the *Observer*, neither did he avoid controversy while preaching. In both jobs, he railed against alcohol, the "filthy weed" known as tobacco, and especially the Roman Catholic Church. In fact, he condemned all Catholics and warned that "Popery" was "spreading in our country to an alarming degree"—no doubt an insult to the Catholics who made up one-third of St. Louis's population. Lovejoy was attracting few defenders.

It was not unusual for reform-minded Protestants of Lovejoy's day to be anti-Catholic. Lyman Beecher (1775-1863), a prominent abolitionist minister and father of Lovejoy's good friend Edward Beecher, warned against a Catholic takeover of the United States.

The *Observer's* stated goal of the "salvation of souls" prompted Lovejoy to take his first real stand against slavery on September 4, 1834. Reacting to an editorial in his former newspaper that called for townspeople to stop local women from teaching Christianity to slaves, Lovejoy argued that slaves had souls "as precious as those of their masters." These were tame words compared to what he soon would print, but Lovejoy's views were emerging.

Seven months later, Lovejoy revealed his growing impatience with slavery. "Something must be done speedily on this all-important subject," he wrote, for God would surely "strike the authors of such cruel oppression." Lovejoy seemed to be begging for a fight. When he narrowly escaped an ambush by proslavery townspeople, he

Abolitionists were horrified by slave auctions, at which infants could be sold away from their mothers and husbands from their wives.

saw his deliverance as the work of God and became more convinced than ever of the righteousness of his position.

Lovejoy addressed his critics in the *Observer*. While he was "threatened with violence and death because I dare to advocate, in any way, the cause of the oppressed," he wrote on November 5, 1835, he could not surrender his principles, "even though my life be the alternative." He would "submit to no such dictation" about what he printed—no matter what the consequences.

The situation rapidly worsened. In December 1835 someone distributed a handbill calling for action to "put down the vile slander of E. P. Lovejoy." The editor wrote his brother that he remained in St. Louis "at the daily peril of my life." But he was most concerned about his family's safety. He had married Celia Ann French less than two years before. Now the controversial editor began to worry that a mob would strike at her and their nine-month-old son, Edward.

Lovejoy's fear of mob violence was justified. In April 1836, four months after the handbill denouncing Lovejoy was circulated, a black cook working aboard a steamboat was burned alive by an enraged St. Louis mob after being accused of murder. When the vigilantes went to trial, Judge Luke Edward Lawless blamed abolitionism, especially Lovejoy and the *Observer*, for inciting the cook to murder. Freedom of the press, Lawless lectured, did not permit one to incite "widespread mischief." Following the judge's logic, the jury found no one guilty of the lynching. Lovejoy, who was a likely target for similar lawlessness, decided in July to move his paper across the Mississippi River to Alton in the free state of Illinois.

Before Lovejoy could move his operation, however, a group of about 20 men broke into the newspaper's warehouse, overturned the printing press, and then hurled other printing equipment into the nearby river. Lovejoy salvaged the press and proceeded with his move to Alton. But within hours of arriving in Illinois on Sunday, July 24, Lovejoy would find out that Alton was no safer than St. Louis. Reluctant to work on the Sabbath, Lovejoy had left his equipment on the dock for the following day. Late that night, a group of men pushed the printing press into the river.

Embarrassed by the event, Alton's leading citizens assured the *Observer*'s outraged editor of their support—if Lovejoy toned down his antislavery message. Since he had "come to a free state where the evil does not exist," Lovejoy agreed, but he quickly reserved the right "to speak, to write, and to publish whatever I please on any subject." The town's officials still stood by him and pledged to pay for a new printing press. By the end of the summer, the *Alton Observer* was in production.

For a while, Lovejoy did take a milder tone against slaveholders. But he still alienated other people who might later have offered support when he needed it. Blistering salvos were aimed at drinkers and Catholics, who together formed a majority of Alton's population. It seemed only a matter of time before Lovejoy would again be the center of controversy.

By early 1837, Lovejoy had resumed his firm antislavery stance. On February 2, he described a plan to send freed slaves to Africa as "utterly inadequate"—a reversal of his earlier, more moderate position. A week later, Lovejoy charged that those who did nothing about slavery were "fighting against God." In the March 16 issue, Lovejoy called for the immediate emancipation of all slaves. His condemnation of Alton's Fourth of July celebration followed a few months later.

In the same issue denouncing the Independence Day festivities, Lovejoy called for the formation of an "Illinois Antislavery Society." Proslavery forces were furious. An abolitionist newspaper was bad enough, but now Lovejoy wanted to form an antislavery organization too!

On the evening of August 21, a mob taunted and threatened Lovejoy as he walked home from a drugstore with medicine for his sick wife. Meanwhile, another group broke into his printing plant and ruined his equipment. Refusing to back down, the editor ordered a third printing press. Alton's mayor hired a guard to watch the new press that arrived on September 21, but a group of men managed to break into the warehouse after the watchman had left and wrecked the machine. "We regret, exceedingly, these violations of the law," the *Missouri Republican* newspaper proclaimed sarcastically from across the river. "If Mr. Lovejoy . . . continues to provoke these attacks," the editorial continued ominously, "they may terminate more disastrously than the mere destruction of property."

A month later, during the last few days of October, Lovejoy invited a friend, abolitionist Edward Beecher, to speak at the Alton church where Lovejoy occasionally preached. Passions flared as Beecher condemned slavery from the pulpit. "If these fanatics will persist," prophesied the *Missouri Republican*, "the already outraged community will [produce] a result to be regretted by all."

On November 3, a group of citizens gathered and passed a resolution silencing Beecher and calling on Lovejoy to leave Alton. The editor rose to object. His right to speak and publish his opinions, he said, "was given me by my Maker, and is solemnly guaranteed to me by the constitution of these United States and of this state." The crowd sat in stony silence as Lovejoy, choked with emotion, vowed not to flee Alton. "No, sir, the contest has commenced here; and here it must be finished. Before God and you all, I here pledge myself to continue it, if need be, until death." At that, Lovejoy turned and left. His fourth—and last—printing press was at that moment sitting on a steamer docked in St. Louis, and he had to make plans to store it.

When the press finally arrived in Alton in the early morning hours of Tuesday, November 7, Lovejoy's supporters quickly pushed it into a nearby warehouse. All remained quiet until later that evening, when a hostile crowd began to gather around the building. Lovejoy and about 15 of his friends prepared a defense against the mob, which had grown to more than 150 people.

The small band inside the warehouse refused to abandon the press. Then, as the crowd surged forward, someone climbed a ladder with a flaming torch. Shots rang out from inside the warehouse, momentarily forcing back the assault. The startled torchbearer dropped to the ground, but he quickly regained his courage and scurried back up the ladder. Lovejoy burst from the building and aimed his pistol at the man setting fire to the roof. As the wood shingles burst into flames, two members of the mob rose from behind cover and fired five shots into Lovejoy. He staggered backward into the warehouse, finally falling dead as fire engulfed the building around him. Elijah Lovejoy's fight was over.

Across the nation, newspapers expressed outrage at the news of Lovejoy's murder. "We shall become the pitiable and despised laughing stock of the world if such desperate acts of bloody tyranny find the support of

A proslavery mob attacks the warehouse in Alton, Illinois, while Lovejoy and his friends protect his printing press.

Americans," lamented the *National Gazette*, a Washington, D.C., newspaper. Horace Greeley, who would become the country's most prominent newspaper editor during the Civil War, criticized "those that talk of Mr. Lovejoy as guilty of resisting public opinion." The *Observer*'s editor had a right to express his opinions, Greeley insisted, even if "five hundred or five thousand" disagreed. Edward Beecher predicted Lovejoy's place in history when he called his departed friend "the first martyr in America to the freedom of speech and the press."

Horace Greeley (1811-1872) was so proud of his newspaper that he hoped his gravestone would read "Founder of The New York Tribune."

2

Horace Greeley
Safeguard of Liberty

Slavery, Horace Greeley believed, was a terrible evil. It could exist only because slaveowners and southern editors forbade a "full and free discussion" of its pros and cons. If the citizens knew all of the facts, surely such an injustice would end. "Liberty of the Press is the palladium [safeguard] of all true Liberty," he wrote in 1848.

Greeley's faith in the power of the press never wavered. The most influential newspaper editor in the United States during the mid-1800s, he believed that in a democracy informed voters could solve most social problems. All that people needed to make the wisest choices

President Abraham Lincoln (1809-1865) changed his views about slavery by listening to new information and arguments, as Greeley had hoped he would.

was accurate information. Greeley used his editorials to educate readers and to prod them into making what he considered to be the correct decisions. In his columns at the height of the Civil War, Greeley was not afraid to criticize even President Abraham Lincoln.

Horace Greeley began life in Amherst, New Hampshire, on February 3, 1811. His parents, Zaccheus and Mary Greeley, were poor farmers. By the time he was 5 years old, Horace had already developed a love for reading. He "devoured newspapers" as he grew and "early resolved to be a printer if I could." When only 11, the ambitious boy met with a printer who needed an *apprentice*—an assistant who learns a trade on the job—but was told he was too young for the work.

Then, in April 1826, 15-year-old Horace landed a position as a printer's apprentice on the staff of the

Northern Spectator, a paper in East Poultney, Vermont. During his apprenticeship, Horace performed many different printing tasks. The most lasting lesson he learned was to give readers the crucial information in the fewest possible words. Concise phrasing was a skill Greeley would later use successfully as an editor.

Horace had what was probably his earliest exposure to slavery during his first year in Vermont. A slave had escaped from nearby New York—where the institution had not yet been completely abolished—and East Poultney townspeople hid the fugitive. After a fruitless search, the slavecatcher went home empty-handed. "Nobody suggested that envy or hate of 'the South,' or of New York, or of the master, had impelled the rescue," Greeley explained. The people simply "hated injustice and oppression" and acted on their beliefs.

Greeley left Vermont in 1830 and looked for work in New York and Pennsylvania. In 1831, he finally found a printer's job in New York City at the one-year-old *New York Evening Post*. He became an editor in 1834, when he founded the weekly *New-Yorker* (no relation to the *New Yorker* magazine published today). The news and literary magazine did reasonably well financially until the economic depression of 1837 sent profits plummeting. To make ends meet over the next few years, Greeley edited the *Jeffersonian* and the *Log Cabin*, two political papers that supported Whig Party candidates.

The Whig Party, predecessor of the Republican Party that would emerge in 1854, supported a strong federal government that could plan and finance such projects as highways and bridges to improve transportation and commercial trade. But the Whigs ran into stiff opposition from the Democrats, who disliked the idea of a powerful central government meddling in their lives.

Whig candidate William Henry Harrison won the presidential election in November 1840, but he died just a month after his inauguration. Although Greeley was distressed, he had learned much from the campaign. In the months before the election, Democrats had appealed to the working-class voters of New York City through two inexpensive newspapers. So Greeley decided to create an affordable paper that would support the Whigs.

Greeley did not endorse every Whig candidate or cause in the daily *New York Tribune*. While he would "openly and heartily advocate the principles" of the Whig Party, Greeley swore he would nevertheless "frankly dissent from its course on a particular question, and even denounce its candidates if they were shown to be deficient in capacity or, far worse, in integrity."

Greeley's paper debuted on April 10, 1841. Despite his experience with the *Jeffersonian*, *Log Cabin*, and the *New-Yorker*, he was still unknown to many readers. But by the end of the first week, daily circulation stood at 2,000. A month and a half later, Greeley's *New York Tribune* reached 10,000 readers every day.

Whig leader Henry Clay was a Greeley favorite because he championed policies to improve the nation's infrastructure, such as roads and canals. Clay also supported steep tariffs on goods from foreign nations to reduce their competition with American products. But

Henry Clay (1777-1852), who was sometimes called the "Great Compromiser" for his role in creating federal legislation that prevented conflicts with the slave states, was unlikely to please Greeley all of the time.

Greeley was vocally antislavery at a time when mainstream Whigs generally tried to ignore the controversial issue. His hero Clay actually owned slaves. The editor also diverged from other Whig policies. Influenced by his experience of poverty while growing up, Greeley promoted ambitious programs to help the poor—including government guarantees of jobs, homes, and education— that upset many of the middle-class businesspeople who supported the Whig Party.

Greeley's *Tribune*—which evolved into daily, weekly, and semiweekly editions—soon attracted a national readership. Alongside the editor's comments on social and political issues were book reviews, reports on national and world developments, and reprints of government documents, such as treaties or bills being considered in

Congress. By the start of the Civil War in 1861, circulation of all editions had grown to 300,000, making the *New York Tribune* the most-read paper in the country.

As the *Tribune*'s popularity exploded in the 1840s, slavery was becoming a major political issue. At the same time that southern planters were turning their sights to new lands in the western United States, northern industrialists also began to look west as they expanded their operations into the midwestern Great Lakes region. The

The editorial staff of the New York Tribune *in the 1840s and 1850s: (seated, left to right) George M. Snow, Bayard Taylor, Horace Greeley, George Ripley; (standing, left to right) William Henry Fry, Charles A. Dana, and Henry J. Raymond.*

nagging problem with westward expansion was whether slavery would be allowed in the new territories.

Because Greeley felt strongly that conflicts could be settled by democratic means, at first he supported legislative attempts to resolve the issue. He accepted most of the Compromise of 1850, which allowed the western territories of Utah and New Mexico to decide by popular vote whether to enter the union as slave or free states.

By 1854, however, Greeley had taken a stand against any law that allowed the extension of slavery. That year, Congress passed Stephen Douglas's Kansas-Nebraska Act, which effectively gave the citizens of *all* prospective states the right to vote whether to allow slavery. No longer would states be accepted only in pairs, one slave and one free, as they had been since the Missouri Compromise of 1820. A vast expansion of slavery was now possible. When he learned the bill was being considered, Greeley warned that "this measure is the first great effort of slavery to take American freedom directly by the throat."

In almost daily attacks lasting from January to May 1854—when President Franklin Pierce signed the bill into law—the *Tribune's* editor called the proposal everything from "measureless treachery and infamy" to one of "the most noxious things ever vegetated on the dung-hill of political corruption." As for the Pierce administration, Greeley declared "that its lack of principle is far excelled by its lack of sense."

Whigs and northern Democrats who were hostile to slavery were also driven to action by the Kansas-Nebraska Act. In 1854, the two groups cooperated to form a new

In the Kansas-Nebraska Act, Stephen A. Douglas (1813-1861) had pushed for "popular sovereignty," or the right for each state's voters to decide whether or not to allow slavery in their state.

party, the Republicans, which denounced slavery. Greeley was thrilled when Republican Abraham Lincoln—who had lost an 1858 Senate bid to Stephen Douglas—won the 1860 presidential election. Although the president-elect vowed to "maintain the Union at all hazards," in a controversial editorial that ran on January 16, 1861, Greeley wrote that if the slave states wanted to leave, then he was "in favor of letting them out as soon as that result can be peacefully and constitutionally attained."

On the issue of slavery's legality, the president and the editor agreed. They hated the institution, but both believed every state had a constitutional right to manage its own internal affairs. Early in 1861, neither supported fighting a war to end slavery.

Despite Lincoln's desire to preserve peace, the Civil War erupted in April 1861 when rebel forces fired on the U.S. Army garrison at Fort Sumter off South Carolina's coast. The federal army's confidence that it would quash the rebellion by the year's end faltered when Southern forces won a crushing victory at Manassas, Virginia, in July 1861. Exhausted from the fighting, the armies settled into defensive positions near Washington, D.C.

When it seceded from the Union in December 1860, South Carolina demanded control of the federal forts in its territory. Several months later, after 34 hours of bombing by the Confederate forces, the commander of Fort Sumter surrendered on April 14, 1861.

Outraged with the administration's handling of the Battle of Manassas, Greeley vented his anger at Lincoln for the "shipwreck of our grand and heroic army." Rival editors, however, claimed Greeley had whipped up public emotion to the point that the president was forced to move before the army had been properly trained. To what degree this was true is not known, but Lincoln clearly recognized Greeley's influence on the public. "Having him firmly behind me," the president admitted, would be as valuable "as an army of one hundred thousand men."

Before Manassas, Greeley had still largely agreed with the president on most issues, especially the reasons for fighting. The editor had written in May 1861, "This war is in truth a war for the preservation of the Union, and not for the destruction of slavery." After Manassas, however, Greeley began to shift his stance.

When one of Lincoln's generals broke with administration policy and issued a proclamation freeing all slaves captured by the Union army, the *Tribune*'s editor refused to denounce the move. Lincoln, on the other hand, ordered the wayward general to reverse the decision.

Soon, Greeley went even one step further than the general. He feared the Confederacy would never be brought to its knees as long as slavery, the "source and mainspring of the rebellion," was still practiced. In an editorial dated December 4, 1861, Greeley pressured Lincoln to emancipate those slaves within Confederate borders if the rebels refused to surrender within a certain amount of time.

The Civil War threatened to rip the nation apart. Well over 600,000 American soldiers died during the war, and nearly as many more lost limbs to amputation.

The president could not afford to ignore Greeley. Without public support, which the powerful editor commanded, the administration could accomplish very little. Greeley's attacks grew more vehement. Any truce that allowed slavery to continue, he wrote on December 20, would be only "brief and hollow." Three weeks later, he complained that he could "not see how the Union and Slavery can both be upheld." In late May, Greeley assured his readers that if slavery was abolished, the remaining issues in the war would "dry up and disappear."

Finally, on August 20, 1862, the *Tribune* carried an editorial addressed to the president. "The Prayer of Twenty Millions," as it was titled, was the most influential column Greeley ever wrote. "We think you are strangely

39

and disastrously remiss in the discharge of your official and imperative duty," the editor began, charging Lincoln with a lack of will to end slavery. Slavery had led to treason, he insisted, and any weakness in dealing with the institution "drives home the wedge intended to divide the Union."

The editor's demand was clear—Lincoln must immediately commit himself to freeing the slaves. In fact, unknown to Greeley or the public, the president had already submitted to his cabinet an initial draft of the Emancipation Proclamation, which would free all slaves in areas still in rebellion on January 1, 1863. Lincoln, who was hoping for a Union victory on the battlefield before publicly releasing the document, was now forced to reconsider his timing.

But first, the president tried to stem the growing public fervor by responding in writing to the editor. Lincoln's letter in the August 22 *Tribune* accomplished little besides giving Greeley another opportunity to plead publicly for an emancipation proclamation. With public opinion clearly mounting behind the editor's position, the president decided to issue the document as soon as he could without damaging the Union army's effort. On September 22, 1862, less than a week after federal forces had fought the rebels to a disappointing draw at the Battle of Antietam, Lincoln released the proclamation.

When the Emancipation Proclamation went into effect on the first day of 1863, Greeley finally got what he wanted—a war to end slavery. It took two more years, but U.S. forces eventually wore down the Confederates, and

This Harper's Weekly *illustration entitled "Emancipation" shows freed black families enjoying the blessings of freedom after escaping the evils of slavery depicted on the left.*

the rebels surrendered on April 9, 1865. Just five days later, President Abraham Lincoln was murdered by John Wilkes Booth.

As the new administration of Andrew Johnson took office, Greeley continued to agitate for reform. Johnson, a Democrat, was a former slaveholder who had run as Lincoln's vice-president in 1864 to broaden support for the Union's war effort. When Johnson opposed granting voting rights to freed black men, Greeley used his editorials to pressure the president to change his mind. In the end, the Republicans' domination of Congress helped them to achieve the vote for black men and other goals.

In 1870, the Fifteenth Amendment to the U.S. Constitution finally guaranteed black men the right to vote. (Black women, like all American women, did not have voting rights until 1920.)

The *Tribune*'s editor, however, did agree with Johnson on granting *amnesty*—or a pardon—to the ex-Confederates. While Greeley had demanded aggressive military action against the South during the war, now he wanted to help the nation reunite. Determined to see everyone participate in government, Greeley could not in good conscience accept the exclusion of Southerners from the political arena.

In 1868, the hero of the Union war effort, General Ulysses S. Grant, defeated his Democratic challenger and became president. Greeley initially supported the new Republican president, but he gradually turned against Grant. By the time the ex-general gave his third annual message to Congress, Greeley complained, "I have had as much of Grant as I can endure!"

Disillusioned with the Grant administration selling political favors, Greeley and other Republicans formed the Liberal Republican Party. The new party chose Greeley to run against Grant in the 1872 presidential election. The *Tribune* editor campaigned enthusiastically, believing the main issue to be a "question of honest men against thieves." Although 2.8 million people voted for

Ulysses S. Grant (1822-1885) pushed through radical Republican legislation, but his administration was riddled with financial and political corruption.

Wanting to "clasp hands across the bloody chasm" left by the Civil War, Greeley hoped his presidency would heal the nation's wounds.

Greeley, Grant won the election handily, with 286 electoral votes to Greeley's 66.

By Election Day, however, Greeley likely no longer cared about the outcome. Just a week before the voting on November 5, Greeley's wife of 36 years, Mary, died after a brief illness. A broken man, Greeley never recovered from the shock, and he died one month later, on November 29, 1872.

To his death, Horace Greeley staunchly defended democracy and freedom of the press. As one of the most widely read journalists during the Civil War, he used his columns to pressure Lincoln to free the slaves at the earliest possible date. The Emancipation Proclamation turned the war into a struggle against slavery. It also ended any chance of foreign intervention on the Southern side because no European country wanted to fight for slavery. At that point, the rebellion was doomed. "The Prayer of Twenty Millions," arguably history's most influential editorial, had solidified Greeley's own legacy as a safeguard of liberty.

Leader of Canada's Reform Party, George Brown (1818-1880) was also a fiercely independent editor. He declared of his Toronto Globe, *"We write to please no man."*

3

George Brown
Canada's Brave Defender

"We hail the birthday of a new nationality," publisher George Brown scribbled hastily on the morning of July 1, 1867. He would have to hurry for the editorial to make the morning edition of his newspaper, the *Toronto Globe*. "A United British America," he continued, "takes its place this day among the nations of the world." It was Dominion Day—the day Ontario, Quebec, Nova Scotia, and New Brunswick combined to form the new nation of Canada—and a crowd was outside anxiously waiting to hear from Brown, the person many historians consider most responsible for the birth of the new nation.

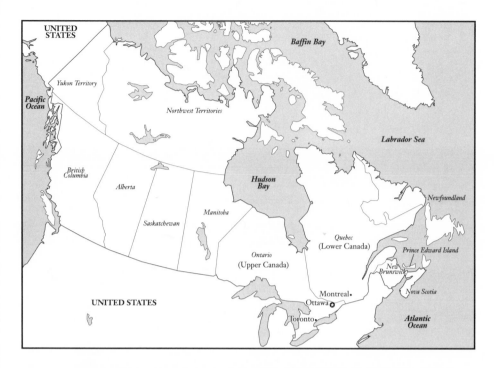

The modern boundaries of Canada. In Brown's day, the British colony of Canada was divided into Upper Canada (now Ontario) and Lower Canada (now Quebec). Nova Scotia, Prince Edward Island, Newfoundland, New Brunswick, and British Columbia were separate British colonies; and what is now Manitoba was owned by the Hudson's Bay Company. The remaining territories had not yet been settled.

This future father of Canada was born in Scotland to Peter and Marianne Brown on November 29, 1818. The Browns lived in Alloa, a tiny port town not far from the city of Edinburgh. After high school, George joined his father's textile business. Working together, father and son discussed books, politics, and the various economic or religious lectures they attended together.

48

In 1837, the Browns were ruined when a depression engulfed the world. The family decided to start over in the United States. Peter and George emigrated in early June 1837 and borrowed money to open a modest drapery shop in New York City. A year later, they were able to send for Marianne and the other children, and the family was reunited in their new home.

As the Browns settled into New York City, Peter began writing political articles in his spare time for the *New York Albion*, a small weekly paper serving the local British community. In his writings, the older Brown often decried the United States' style of democracy that allowed a simple majority of people—even uneducated workers and farmers—to make laws. Such "democracy"

Peter and Marianne Brown. While Peter was the descendant of farmers, Marianne could trace her lineage back to English kings John and Edward I.

amounted to "tyranny of the majority," he argued, which actually denied freedom to those in the minority. Peter also criticized slavery, an institution he believed made a mockery of America's claim of freedom.

The British system, Peter Brown pronounced, was far better. While limiting the power of the monarch, the parliamentary system also prevented what Brown called "mob rule." In England, even the upper-middle classes had only had the right to vote since 1832. Peter's articles were so popular among British and Scottish immigrants as well as antislavery northerners that he decided to publish a paper of his own. George worked with him.

The first issue of the four-page *British Chronicle* appeared on July 30, 1842. To increase circulation, George traveled throughout New England and what was then known as Upper and Lower Canada (now Ontario and Quebec). The younger Brown had grown weary of what he felt was America's hostility to the British and fell in love with Canada. Writing that Canada was "young" and offered fame and wealth to the ambitious, George convinced his father to move their newspaper to the growing city of Toronto in July 1843.

The Browns introduced their paper—renamed the *Banner*—on August 18, 1843. In the four-page foldout, Peter reported on religious matters while George handled political issues. Gordon Brown, George's 15-year-old brother, served as an apprentice.

In his political articles, George aligned the *Banner* with the Reform Party, a group fighting for *responsible government*, or self-government, in the British colony of

Canada. The reformers wanted the governor-general—the British crown's chief administrator in Canada—to be more responsive to the colonial assembly. Brown felt such a system would prove a "happy medium between absolute monarchy on the one hand and the tyranny of a democratic majority on the other."

As the *Banner*'s circulation passed 1,700 by February 1844, George Brown's political support became critical. Reform leaders offered to help him finance a new Reform Party newspaper. Eager to concentrate on politics, Brown jumped at the chance. The 25-year-old began publishing the weekly *Toronto Globe* in March 1844.

Brown sunk his profits into faster presses and better printing facilities. By 1849, the *Globe* had grown from a

Since 1836 Robert Baldwin (1804-1858) had led the drive for responsible government. He served two terms as the prime minister of Upper Canada, 1842-1843 and 1847-1851.

tiny weekly with an initial audience of 300 readers to a paper that reached 4,000 Canadians three times a week. Brown pushed his influence further west in October 1845, adding the *Western Globe* edition. Since the *Toronto Globe's* endorsements had helped Reformers win control of the government in January 1848, they repaid Brown by naming the *Globe* the government's official paper. Within five years of the *Globe's* first issue, Brown had become not only Toronto's leading publisher, but also a power in Canadian politics.

After winning self-government in 1848, Canadians moved on to another controversial question: Should their country become part of the United States? This annexation issue had emerged in 1846 when Great Britain's repeal of the Corn Laws—tariffs on imported wheat (which the British call "corn")—reduced the artificially high price Canadian wheat farmers earned for their crops. Canadian conservatives, called *Tories*, believed the only way for their country to survive was to merge with the economically powerful United States. At the other political extreme, radical members of Brown's own Reform Party also pushed for annexation in order to be part of America's democratic political system.

Believing Canada was destined for greatness, Brown detested the idea of uniting with its southern neighbor. The Tories had "gone demented" for even suggesting it, he fumed. With well-reasoned arguments, Brown tore into the annexationists. Why should Canada, the *Globe* asked, want to join a country that spoke of freedom while allowing slavery? Furthermore, America's voting laws allowed the most ignorant and vicious of men to help determine the course of the nation.

As the economy rebounded by the end of 1849, the cry for union with the United States had largely fallen silent. But the radical elements within the Reform Party—called "Clear Grits"—still hoped to create a democracy where *all* leaders faced election and government must answer to the people.

Brown continued to oppose the democracy movement, but in Grit leader William McDougall he had found a powerful opponent. The editor of the *North American*, the Grit newspaper, McDougall charged that George Brown was nothing more than a "mean, quibbling, degraded traitor" for opposing the Clear Grits.

As the Reform government's official paper, the *Globe*'s opposition to the Grits was understandable. But Brown was no blind follower of the government. He split with the party in July 1851 over the church-state issue of *voluntaryism*. Churches should depend solely on voluntary contributions of their members, he argued, and never receive support or sanction from the state. Brown felt the government was allowing the Catholic Church too great a say in the making of government policy. It was a stance—the first of many as it would turn out—shared by the Clear Grits.

The publisher felt so strongly about the issue that he decided to voice his opposition as a member of parliament. Leaving his younger brother Gordon in charge of the *Globe* in November 1851, Brown campaigned and won the election on a platform of separation of church

In 1851, Brown decided to run for parliament in order to focus attention on voluntary contributions to churches as "the great issue at the coming election."

and state, free trade with the United States, and representation by population in parliament—an issue that would soon eclipse the church-state controversy.

The notion of "rep by pop," as it was called, had been around since 1841, when the Act of Union joined Upper and Lower Canada into one province served by a single parliament. Despite the fact that Lower Canada had the greater population at the time of union, it was limited to the same number of seats in parliament as Upper Canada. Now, as the 1851 census revealed a sharp population shift to Upper Canada, it was *that* section that clamored for a proportional increase in representation.

While Brown wasn't the first to suggest representation by population, he was the first to call for rep by pop "without regard to a separating line between Upper

Canada and Lower." In other words, he wanted a more unified nation with representation based on the population. Although Brown's March 1853 proposal was defeated, it was the first step toward creating a truly united Canadian nation.

By the end of 1853, Brown had expanded the *Toronto Globe* into a daily with a circulation of 8,000, more than any of the 13 other newspapers serving Toronto's 35,000 residents. Along with the weekly edition published in Upper Canada's western regions, the *Western Globe*, the *Globe* enabled Brown to reach a huge number of potential voters with his legislative message.

The next parliamentary elections were slated for July 1854. Following his victory, Brown set to work building a coalition composed of lawmakers loyal to him and the other dominant group in Upper Canadian politics—the Clear Grits, his former enemies. This coalition would work toward the achievement of goals they shared in common.

While they still disagreed on many issues, the two groups both sought rep by pop and the separation of church and state. As Grit leader William McDougall observed, all the reformers needed to "row in the same boat" if they hoped for success. Brown and the Grits had much to offer each other. With the support of Upper Canada's large rural population, the Clear Grits were the stronger faction. But Brown's supporters were fiercely loyal, and with Upper Canada's biggest newspaper operation, he could give the new coalition the means to reach even greater numbers.

Not long after the Clear Grits joined forces with the Reformers, William McDougall (1822-1905) sold the North American *to Brown and became part of the* Globe's *staff of talented and influential writers.*

By the summer of 1855, George Brown controlled a revamped Reform Party. In the words of one historian, "the party would be grounded on the *Globe*'s platform." As the publisher turned profits back into the *Globe*—a new press here, a bigger building there—the paper grew. Circulation surpassed 18,000 by 1856, giving Brown a huge base of support.

Brown's backing of rep by pop and his defiance of Catholic-dominated Lower Canada made him wildly popular in Upper Canada. To his surprise, he was asked to run for parliament in the conservative stronghold of Toronto instead of the safe Reform seat he'd held before. (Candidates could run for office in any *riding*, or district, whether they lived there or not.) His supporters sang his campaign song, "The People's Champion," in the streets: "The whole of the land and he were one! Hurrah for our brave defender!" The "brave defender" won the 1857 election handily, and the Reform Party coalition now dominated the politics of Upper Canada.

In July 1858, just six months after Brown took office, a series of events made him the prime minister. When parliament rejected Queen Victoria's recommendation to make Ottawa the capital city, the Liberal-Conservative Coalition government of John A. Macdonald and George Cartier resigned to protest the insult to the queen. As leader of the opposition Reform Party, George Brown was appointed the new prime minister, along with Lower Canadian Antoine Aimé Dorion. The two put together a remarkable new government representing both Lower and Upper Canada, Catholics as well as Protestants.

But the Brown-Dorion government was crushed. Its plan for representation by population with constitutional protections for the outnumbered Catholics would not come to fruition. Since the British governor-general would not allow new elections, the Reform leaders' hands were tied with a parliament dominated by Macdonald's Liberal-Conservative Coalition. Brown's government had little choice but to resign after just two days in office.

Depressed with the setback to the Reform Party, Brown began endorsing the dissolution of the union of Upper and Lower Canada. But he soon recovered and devoted himself anew to the federation of the British colonies of North America. The prospect of the spread of Canada to the West, even all the way to the Pacific Coast, sparked his passion. In 1856, the *Globe* had called for the takeover of "the vast and fertile territory which is our birthright—and which no power on earth can prevent us occupying."

The Upper Canadian Reform Party convention of November 1859 made the federation of Upper and Lower Canada a party plank for the first time. At the dawn of 1860, the *Globe* expressed its faith "that Canada contains within herself elements of progress which will yet place her among the foremost nations of the world." But Brown failed to convince Lower Canada to accept the Reform Party's proposal for federation under an ill-defined "joint authority." The Toronto citizens lost faith in him and voted him out of parliament in 1861.

Brown was thrilled with the defeat of John A. Macdonald and George Cartier's Liberal-Conservative Coalition government in April 1862. But the Reform government that succeeded it had to compromise to stay in power. The new premier from Upper Canada, John Sandfield Macdonald, a longstanding Upper Canadian Reform Party member, opposed rep by pop. "Are you all mad there?" telegraphed an incensed Brown when he learned his Reform Party associates in the new government had agreed not to pursue rep by pop.

Brown decided he must return to parliament in 1863 to fight for rep by pop. The government of John Sandfield Macdonald and Lower Canadian Louis Sicotte was soon in crisis and had to be reorganized. When Macdonald came to him for help, Brown advised him to choose Antoine Dorion—who had served as premier with

Brown for those two days in 1858—as leader of Lower Canada. Brown hoped the new government would finally consider rep by pop.

The elections of 1863 showed how divided the "union" of Canada was. Upper Canada, tired of being ruled by Lower Canada, turned decidedly toward the Reform Party. But Lower Canada, determined to maintain its advantage in representation, voted out many Reform Party members. Upper Canada and Lower Canada were in a deadlock over the issue of representation, and the Macdonald-Dorion government crumbled.

After the collapse of the government, Brown's old enemy John A. Macdonald approached him in June 1864. Macdonald wanted Brown to help save the Canadian union. The seemingly impossible happened: George

Although Brown admitted he had opposed John A. Macdonald (1815-1891) "in the most hostile manner it is possible to conceive," he felt the state of the Canadian union warranted such desperate measures.

Brown became president of the cabinet in the government of Etienne Taché and John A. Macdonald. This "Great Coalition" would create a new Canada.

To explain his willingness to join a coalition with his longtime political foes, Brown stated, "if a crisis has ever arisen in the political affairs of any country which would justify a coalition, such a crisis has arrived in the history of Canada." Not only was the existing Canadian union threatened, but the British colonies were also concerned about the United States. The United States was challenging Canadian rights to western settlements, and the Americans' growing economic power was damaging Canadian trade. In addition, Canada was being drawn into the American Civil War as Confederate forces made attacks on the Union army from Canadian soil.

As president of the new cabinet, Brown set to work to create a federated union of British North America. He sought to avoid the system of government that had allowed states in the United States to rebel against their central government in the Civil War. In the confederation of British North America, provincial governments would be small and limited to specified functions. Unlike the American system, in which states retain all rights not given to the central government, the central government in Canada would retain all rights not given to the states.

The new Canadian parliament would be modeled on the British parliament. As in the British House of Lords, the Canadian Senate would be composed of leaders nominated by the prime minister. But the lower house would enjoy the long-sought representation by population.

It became too difficult, however, for Brown to keep collaborating with conservatives in the new government. In December 1865, he resigned his cabinet position over the issue of trade relations with the United States. The conservative-dominated cabinet had, in his view, granted Canada's southern neighbor too many trade concessions.

While Brown remained in parliament, he prepared for his return to full-time journalism. In 1866, he incorporated his holdings as the Globe Printing Company, which included the *Toronto Globe*, the *Evening Globe*, the

The Globe building, topped by a globe, on Toronto's King Street in 1868

Weekly Globe, and the *Canada Farmer*. As he told a fellow Reformer, "party leadership and the conducting of a great journal don't harmonize." Brown no longer wanted to tailor his writing to the needs of the Reform Party.

After his retirement from parliament, Brown devoted himself to the *Globe* papers. He bought new printing presses and revamped the *Toronto Globe* with brand-new type and wire-service reports from Europe, the United States, and other parts of Canada. He also enlarged the *Canada Farmer* and opened *Globe* branch offices in other Canadian cities. By 1869, all of the *Globe* editions combined had a circulation of nearly 48,000.

It was the success of confederation—Brown's long-time dream—that drew the newspaper editor back into politics. On March 29, 1867, the British parliament passed the British North America Act for the "Dominion of Canada," composed of Ontario (Upper Canada), Quebec (Lower Canada), Nova Scotia, and New Brunswick. (Canada purchased new territories in 1869, and in 1870 Manitoba joined the confederation. British Columbia was added in 1871, Prince Edward Island in 1873, Alberta and Saskatchewan in 1905, and Newfoundland in 1949.) The nation of Canada was born.

In Brown's view, since confederation had been achieved, the Coalition government was no longer necessary. So he busied himself rebuilding the neglected Reform Party. After the Upper Canadian Reform Party convention in June 1867, Brown was persuaded to run for parliament once again for the sake of the Reform Party. Brown decided to run in South Ontario, east of Toronto, in an area where the Reform Party was not strong. His presence, he thought, would help the Reform cause in the eastern sections of Ontario. But the Coalition campaigned hard against Brown, and the Reform Party leader lost the late August election. With Reformers losing almost everywhere else as well, the Coalition of John A. Macdonald had cemented its power in the new nation.

Canada remained politically fickle, with the Reform Party trouncing the Coalition in 1872 and then being routed in the 1878 elections. Tired of politics, Brown devoted himself to his farm and his newspapers. He began revamping the *Globe* papers again, turning the *Toronto Globe* into an eight-page paper instead of a four-page foldout and expanding the *Weekly Globe* as well. He bought two brand-new printing presses that could print, cut, and fold 28,000 *Globe*s per hour.

As it turned out, Canada's "brave defender" needed a defender himself. An unknown arsonist twice burned barns on Brown's country estate. Set back by these attacks and investments in the *Globe* papers, Brown was financially strapped by the end of 1879 and lost his farm. The publisher was preoccupied with these concerns on the afternoon of March 25, 1880, when a disgruntled *Toronto Globe* employee came into his office. After a brief struggle, the man shot Brown. Although the leg wound was only superficial, it became severely infected. On May 9, 1880, George Brown died, believing—wrongly—that he had left his family in financial ruin.

After William Randolph Hearst (1863-1951) took over the San Francisco Examiner *in 1887, he made it the "Monarch of the Dailies."*

4

William Randolph Hearst
The "Yellowist" Journalist

"*We* don't want fine writing in a newspaper," Sam Chamberlain, the *San Francisco Examiner*'s managing editor, told his new reporter—"Remember that." The young woman stared in confusion as her boss continued his lecture. Every morning, he said, there's a police officer, shopkeeper, or trolley-car operator who sits down for a few minutes to read the paper. "Think of him when you're writing a story," declared Chamberlain. "Don't write a single line he can't understand and wouldn't read." Great writing might win a slew of awards, he reminded her, but only easy-to-read and attention-grabbing stories *sold* papers. And for the *Examiner*'s owner, William Randolph Hearst, nothing else mattered.

Hearst used every trick to lure readers. Splashy illustrations and banner headlines enlivened stories, and sensational tales of scandal and murder grabbed readers' attention. Sometimes Hearst even pulled fantastic stories out of thin air. His exaggerated and often fictional newspaper accounts of Spanish treachery and torture in Cuba in the late-1890s, for instance, caused such a furor that Congress was forced to declare war on Spain. To Hearst, truth was important *only* if it increased circulation.

William Randolph Hearst was born in San Francisco, California, on April 29, 1863. His father, George Hearst, was a miner who had struck it rich in 1859. Soon afterward, the new millionaire had married Phoebe Apperson, a schoolteacher.

The Hearsts' only child, William grew up the center of his mother's loving attention. Whatever he wanted, Phoebe Hearst provided. Young "Willie" was raised with every advantage—opera, art museums, and the best education money could buy. In 1882, the 19-year-old entered Harvard University, the oldest and one of the most prestigious colleges in the nation.

Unfortunately, William never applied himself to his studies. He dreamed instead of finding fabulous riches like his father had. Halfway through his second year at Harvard, William had gained notoriety for his ability to spring practical jokes on unsuspecting professors and for feeding liquor to his pet alligator—whom he called Champagne Charlie.

William was desperately homesick at Harvard, writing to his mother, "I shall never live anywhere but in California."

Around this time, William developed enthusiasm for something constructive for the first time in his life. A friend needed help raising money for the *Harvard Lampoon*, the university's humor magazine. What the friend wanted was funding from William's wealthy father, but William had something else in mind. He sold advertising space in the *Lampoon* to local businesses and then led a successful drive to increase circulation. As more people read the *Lampoon*, more businesses bought advertising space. For the first time, the magazine began to show a profit—and William had discovered his calling.

Hearst now began reading all the major newspapers he could get his hands on, studying their writing styles and overall appeal. His favorite was the *New York World*, the paper Joseph Pulitzer had purchased in 1883. Hearst admired the way Pulitzer generated sales by targeting his newspaper to a mass readership. Sensational subjects such as murder—complete with lurid drawings of the crime scene—were heavily reported, as were investigations of business monopolies and political corruption. In only three years, the *World*'s circulation rose from 15,000 to 250,000, making it the largest of any newspaper in the country.

William hoped to convince his father that he could run the paper George Hearst had acquired in 1880: the *San Francisco Examiner*. Although the *Examiner* was a huge money loser, young Hearst believed he could turn it around. But William knew almost nothing about running newspapers and needed a job with a paper to learn the business. After Harvard finally expelled him after one prank too many, William found work with Pulitzer's *World* in late 1885.

Hearst learned firsthand from Pulitzer about the power of the press. The Statue of Liberty, a gift from France commemorating its alliance with the United States during the American Revolution, had arrived in New York in 1885. Unfortunately, it lay in pieces because Congress refused to authorize enough money for a base. Through the *World*, Pulitzer launched a fundraising campaign. Within five months, he had collected the amount necessary to erect the statue. Hearst never forgot Pulitzer's use of the *World* to call the public to action.

In January 1887, Hearst finally got his shot at running the *Examiner* after George Hearst won election to

Joseph Pulitzer (1847-1911) taught Hearst tactics to grab the public's attention, but he also cared about journalistic quality. In his will, the publisher endowed the Pulitzer Prize for excellence in journalism.

the U.S. Senate. "I am anxious to begin work," Hearst wrote his father, boldly predicting that within a year "our circulation will have increased ten thousand." The *Examiner* would succeed by being "alarmingly enterprising" and "startlingly original." Within five years, Hearst boasted, "we will be the biggest paper on the Pacific slope." The senator, who had already lost a quarter-million dollars on the paper, scoffed at what he considered more of his son's foolishness.

Beginning with the March 4 issue, Hearst set about revolutionizing the *Examiner*. With circulation stagnant at just under 24,000, the new boss initiated several innovations to attract more readers. He increased the size of headlines; enlarged local, national, and world news coverage; inserted columns of society gossip; and, in a move considered especially undignified by the *Examiner's* veteran editors, transferred sports news to the first page.

When Hearst's main competitor, the *San Francisco Chronicle*, scooped the *Examiner* with a report of a fire, Hearst produced a 14-page special edition, or *extra*, on the blaze. Laced with brilliant illustrations and huge headlines, the sensational descriptions gripped readers, and sales of the extra skyrocketed even though the *Chronicle* had covered the story first.

Soon the *Examiner* itself was turning up in headlines all over the country. Pulitzer's *World* called it a "live newspaper of the present era," while the *Chicago Tribune* praised Hearst for shaking up "the dry bones of newspaperdom in San Francisco."

Hearst loved every aspect of newspaper production. He set type for the printing press, came up with story ideas, and wrote dozens of eye-catching headlines. He lived and breathed the news, and his enthusiasm infected everyone in the newsroom. But a love of the news did not translate into a love for truth. Through the years, as he built an empire that eventually included 9 magazines and 18 newspapers in 12 cities, Hearst's highest priority always remained increased readership. He was even willing to stage news stories to entice readers. One reporter, hoping to write an exposé about mental institutions, purposely acted insane after jumping from a steamboat. He was promptly institutionalized and wrote about his experiences in the asylum.

By March 1888, a year after Hearst had taken over the *Examiner*, the paper's daily sales stood at 40,000. Three years later, circulation soared past the 57,000 mark, making it the most-read paper in the city. With a year to spare, William Hearst had achieved the goals he had outlined to his father four years earlier.

In 1895, four years after her husband's death, Phoebe Hearst sold the family's mines. Ever the giving mother, she turned the $7,500,000 over to her son. William Hearst used part of the money to expand his budding publishing empire to the East Coast by purchasing the *Morning Journal*, the worst-selling daily in New York City.

When Hearst moved into the *Journal*'s offices in September, the paper reached only 77,000 readers a day. In contrast, Joseph Pulitzer's *World* had daily sales of 500,000. By the end of the year, however, the *Journal*'s readership had climbed past 100,000. Again, the secret rested in Hearst's appeal to the masses. Like Pulitzer, he reported sensational crimes and scandal. And to capture the *World*'s readers, Hearst dropped the price of his paper to a penny, half of what Pulitzer's paper cost. Although Hearst initially lost money, he didn't care as long as circulation rose.

The publisher tirelessly pursued new readers. Billboard advertisements hung from rafters in railroad stations and on streetcars. Pennies by the barrel were mailed to potential readers. To improve his paper while hurting the others, Hearst repeated an old trick used with success in San Francisco—he offered high salaries to the competition's best talent. By February 1896, 150,000 copies of the *Journal* were purchased every day, forcing Pulitzer to halve the *World*'s price to compete.

As the circulation war heated up, an incident took place that gave birth to the phrase "yellow journalism." While raiding Pulitzer's staff, Hearst snagged the cartoonist who drew a popular strip called "The Yellow Kid," named for a mischievous youth who wore a yellow nightshirt. Pulitzer struck back by hiring another artist to continue drawing the cartoon for the *World*. Eventually, as the two troublemaking kids competed for readers, other papers began labeling the battle "yellow journalism." The term soon came to mean the sensational style of news reporting practiced by Hearst and Pulitzer.

The newspaper battle continued through the hotly contested 1896 presidential campaign between William Jennings Bryan and William McKinley. Hearst's was the lone paper in the East to support Bryan, a Democrat who had caused a split in his party by supporting "free silver," the unlimited production of coins to increase money flowing into the economy. Since most of Bryan's followers turned to the *Journal*, readership soared. Immediately after the election—which Bryan lost—circulation of Hearst's *Journal* peaked at 1,300,000 copies. In just over a year, sales had grown more than tenfold, making the *Journal* the second-most-read paper in the United States. Only Pulitzer's *New York World*—whose circulation had also dramatically increased—claimed a bigger audience.

But it would not be long before Hearst discovered a way to finally overcome his old nemesis. On the island of

After his loss in 1896, William Jennings Bryan (1860-1925) would run two more times—in 1900 and 1908—on his "free silver" platform, but he never was elected president.

Cuba, 90 miles off the southern tip of Florida, rebels had been battling for independence from Spain since 1895. American public support leaned heavily toward the rebels, who were viewed as brutalized freedom fighters mainly because of stories about Spanish atrocities published in the *Journal* and other papers—reports that could not be authenticated because of the tight restrictions the Spaniards placed on news correspondents.

Hearst didn't care whether his reports were true. In 1897, he sent famed artist Frederic Remington to the island to illustrate the heated action. But as far as Remington could tell, everything was quiet in Cuba. "I wish to return," he told Hearst. Don't worry, said his boss. "You furnish the pictures and I'll furnish the war."

Hearst kept his word. Across the top of one *Journal* story stretched the headline: "FEEDING PRISONERS TO SHARKS." Another report accused Spanish troops of regularly beating their Cuban prisoners to death. Yet another story recounted how three Cuban girls were stripped naked by Spanish officers searching for secret documents—a tale that Pulitzer's *World* soon proved had been grossly exaggerated by the *Journal*.

Together the nation's major prowar papers—most notably the *Journal*, the *World*, and the *New York Sun*—reached millions of readers throughout the country. With such a wide audience constantly digesting a stream of inflammatory information, a violent outburst of indignation had to follow.

The explosion finally came on February 15, 1898. Anchored in the port of Havana, Cuba, the U.S. Navy's *Maine* blew apart, killing 260 sailors. While the cause of the blast still remains a mystery, to Hearst the Spanish were clearly to blame. "THE WARSHIP *MAINE* WAS SPLIT IN TWO BY AN ENEMY'S SECRET INFERNAL MACHINE," blared a *Journal* headline two days later. Even though President McKinley himself believed the ship's demise had been caused by an accidental explosion of ammunition, Hearst refused to back off, and the

Like Hearst's Journal, *Pulitzer's* World *showed graphic images of the sinking* Maine *and called for action.*

Journal urged its readers to demand that their representatives in Congress vote for war.

On April 19, the U.S. Congress gave Hearst what he wanted—a declaration of war on Spain. "NOW TO AVENGE THE *MAINE*," trumpeted the *Journal* in four-inch type. Revenge was quick and severe. By the end of July, two Spanish fleets—one near Cuba and the other in the Philippines in the Pacific Ocean—lay at the bottom of the ocean. Resistance on land had ended earlier in the month with the Americans' decisive victory at the Battle

The fighting in the Spanish-American War was brief and ill-matched as U.S. troops quickly overran the outnumbered Spanish forces in Cuba.

of San Juan Hill. The United States had come into possession of a brand-new empire, and Hearst had finally caught up with Pulitzer in newspaper sales—never mind that it had taken a war to do so.

A few years later, President William McKinley was fatally shot by an assassin on September 6, 1901. The new president, Theodore Roosevelt, placed some of the blame for McKinley's murder on "the reckless utterances" of people, including journalists, who had stirred up hatred. Few doubted that Roosevelt had been referring to Hearst, who had printed vociferous attacks on McKinley in his newspapers. Partly to deflect criticism, Hearst changed the name of the *Morning Journal* to the *New York American*. He had earlier launched the *Chicago American* in 1900 and would launch yet another paper by that name, the *Boston American*, in 1904.

While he busily spread his publishing empire, Hearst won back-to-back elections to Congress as a New York representative in 1902 and 1904. His attempt to gain the Democratic presidential nomination in 1904, however, met with defeat. Other campaigns—to become mayor of New York City in 1905 and to win the governorship of New York in 1906—ended in failure as well.

William McKinley (1843-1901), reelected in 1900, had barely served six months of his second term when he was killed by an anarchist who called him "an enemy of good working people."

Hearst's greatest successes remained in publishing. In the summer of 1905, he purchased *Cosmopolitan*, one of the nation's most popular magazines. With his usual enthusiasm, he dived into the investigative journalism known as *muckraking*. The staff of *Cosmopolitan* uncovered evidence proving a U.S. senator was on the payroll of a big insurance company while in a position to enact laws favorable to the firm. According to the exposé, the problem was that senators were not directly elected by the people, but rather by their state's legislatures. As a result, the people could not hold senators accountable. The *Cosmopolitan* story contributed to a public outcry that six years later led to passage of the Seventeenth Amendment, which took the power to choose senators away from the state legislatures and gave it directly to the people.

When World War I began in 1914, Hearst surprisingly avoided the fighting words he had employed 16 years earlier to nudge the United States into war against Spain. In fact, he tried to keep his country from any involvement in Europe. Failing to demonize the unpopular Germans was all the more strange because it cost Hearst circulation. But Hearst distrusted the British, who, in a desperate attempt to lure the U.S. into the war, were spreading their own unproven charges about German brutality. The newly peaceful Hearst eventually lost his battle to keep America out of the conflict when President Woodrow Wilson convinced Congress to declare war against the Germans in 1917.

By the time Hearst was 60 in 1923, his ability to generate circulation was unrivaled. The publisher boasted one of the world's top yearly incomes at over $12 million. He had even ventured into the hot new film industry. Hearst's reputation as a journalist, however, could have fallen no lower. "A blazing disgrace to the craft," said one magazine of him, while New York governor Al Smith declared, "You cannot look for truth" in Hearst's papers.

Hearst owned more than 30 newspapers by 1930, with a combined daily readership of 11 million. His magazines included *Good Housekeeping*, *Harper's Bazaar*, and *Ladies' Home Journal*—all of them top sellers to this day.

Marion Davies became involved with Hearst in 1917, when she was dancing in the Ziegfeld Follies. By 1919, he had hatched a plan to make her a movie star and become a film tycoon himself in the process.

But all was not well with Hearst's empire. Although he made incredible amounts of money, he spent even more. As 1937 rolled around, Hearst was losing so much money he had to give up financial control of his publications. New managers cracked down on waste and sold several papers, magazines, and unprofitable real-estate holdings. Also axed was his motion-picture enterprise, which he had started with the hope of making his mistress, Marion Davies, a star. Even after these drastic steps, only the onset of World War II in 1939—with the advertising revenue and increased circulation it generated—saved Hearst from financial disaster.

Compounding Hearst's financial embarrassments was Orson Welles's 1941 movie *Citizen Kane*, which many critics consider one of the best films of all time. The film told the life of Charles Foster Kane, millionaire newspaper publisher. Like Hearst, Kane had built a fabulous castle on California's coastline to house his famous art collection. And, like Hearst, Kane had left his wife for a beautiful and not very talented young performer. The portrayal of Marion Davies especially infuriated Hearst. The publisher forbid his papers from reviewing the film or any other R.K.O. production, and he tried to prevent the film's distribution as well. But, despite Hearst's efforts, *Citizen Kane* was wildly successful.

The stress wore on Hearst. Following the end of World War II in 1945, his health began to fail. The publisher suffered a heart attack in 1947. Four years later, on August 14, 1951, William Randolph Hearst died at the age of 88.

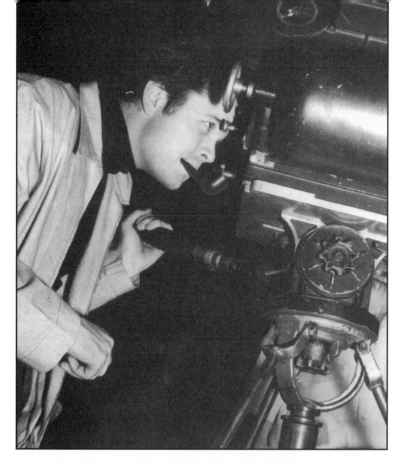

Orson Welles (1915-1985) was only in his twenties when he wrote, directed, produced, and starred in Citizen Kane. *Today, he is still considered one of the world's greatest filmmakers.*

Hearst's legacy will always be associated with "yellow journalism." During his obsessive quest for readership that led the United States into war against Spain in 1898, truth was never Hearst's priority. Instead, circulation, and with it profit and power, drove the publisher. He owed his overwhelming success to his ability to tap into the mind of the common reader and to make innovations that have forever altered the face of journalism.

Ida Tarbell (1857-1944) was called the "Joan of Arc of the Oil Regions" for her exposé of the monopolistic business practices of the Standard Oil Company.

5

Ida M. Tarbell
The Meticulous Muckraker

*P*resident Theodore Roosevelt was angry. Every day another article about corruption and illegal activity was appearing in the newspapers. Journalists who reported only the dark side of politics and big business, the president thundered in April 1906, were like the "man with the muckrake" in the classic book *Pilgrim's Progress*. That man refused to look up from the ground as he raked "to himself the filth of the floor." Filth, or corruption, should be exposed, but the reporter who does nothing else "speedily becomes . . . one of the most potent forces of evil" in the country. Investigative journalism, warned the

Even though President Theodore Roosevelt (1858-1919) complained about the excesses of the "muckrakers," he led the charge against business corruption and for reforms to protect consumers.

president, was only beneficial when held to rigorous standards of accuracy.

Ida Tarbell, one of the first "muckrakers," as they came to be called, agreed that journalists should strive for truth. Her landmark articles detailed the way John D. Rockefeller's Standard Oil Company had gained a *monopoly*, or sole control, over the oil industry. According to one historian, her series was "one of the greatest serials ever to appear in an American magazine." Tarbell's exposé made her famous and established a model for investigative journalism that is still followed today.

Ida Minerva Tarbell was born in Erie County, Pennsylvania, on November 5, 1857. Her parents, Esther and Franklin Tarbell, were schoolteachers. But after oil was discovered in Pennsylvania, Franklin seized the opportunity and moved the family to Rouseville, a town not far from where oil had been found in Titusville.

Franklin developed a wooden storage tank for oil that proved a hit with the oil-well owners. In 1870, the now-prosperous family moved to Titusville to be closer to the booming industry.

In 1872, profits for Titusville's small oil producers suddenly dried up when the railroads that shipped the oil doubled their rates. While Titusville's producers suffered, a mammoth company controlled by millionaire

Workers pose with early oil-drilling machinery in northwestern Pennsylvania after the 1859 discovery of oil in that area.

John D. Rockefeller actually received money *back* from the railroads because the bigger company shipped so much oil. A sense of injustice spread through town, creating in Ida "a hatred of privilege—privilege of any sort."

Another powerful influence on Ida was her mother. Esther often welcomed into the Tarbell home reformers working for women's rights. Meeting these women convinced Ida of the importance of financial independence for women. So she promised herself that she would get an education and avoid marriage. In autumn 1876, the young woman enrolled in Allegheny College in Meadville, Pennsylvania.

At Allegheny, the energetic Ida edited the school paper; participated in a literary society that discussed current events, philosophy, and history; and evolved into a formidable public speaker. After graduating in the spring of 1880, she quickly found a job teaching high-school students in Poland, Ohio.

Tarbell dived into her first real job, teaching classes in four languages—German, French, Latin, and Greek—as well as science and math. Having loved to study rock fragments under her microscope as a child, Tarbell especially enjoyed showing her students the scientific process in lab work. From science, she learned the importance of gathering sound facts before drawing conclusions.

Because of insufficient pay, Tarbell gave up teaching after two years and moved back into her parents' home. It was a fortunate move. Through her parents, Tarbell met a man named Theodore L. Flood, founder and editor of the *Chautauquan*, a monthly magazine published in nearby

Meadville. Impressed by the bright young woman, Flood convinced Tarbell to join his staff in 1883. "To me it was only a temporary thing," she remembered. "I had no inclination toward writing or toward editorial work."

Tarbell worked at her "temporary" job as an editor and writer for the *Chautauquan* for the next seven years. On the job, she perfected her keen attention to detail. Tarbell remembered worrying, "What if the accent was in the wrong place? What if I brought somebody into the world in the wrong year?"

At this time, the world outside the Meadville newsroom was far from calm. In May 1886, a riot broke out in Chicago's Haymarket Square when a bomb exploded amid 1,500 labor demonstrators. What had begun several days earlier as a march for an 8-hour workday ended with 11 dead and 100 wounded activists. Tarbell supported the 8-hour workday (workers at the time often worked 10 to 12 hours) and at her urging Flood began to publish more articles pushing social and economic reform. Tarbell's philosophy was simple—businesses should apply the Golden Rule, treating their workers and customers as they themselves would prefer to be treated.

While in Meadville, Tarbell also learned three basic characteristics of good journalism. First, balanced coverage requires the presentation of all sides of an issue. Next, the information must be clearly and completely explained. Finally, only accurate reporting instills readers' trust in a publication.

In 1890, Tarbell decided to leave the *Chautauquan* because her duties as editor prevented her from writing about the subjects that most interested her. She wanted a new challenge and craved adventure. After meeting with newspaper editors from Pittsburgh, Cincinnati, and other regional cities, Tarbell convinced them to buy articles that she would write—from Paris!

By August 1891, Tarbell's articles from the French capital were running in American papers. Her first features described the culture of Paris—a hot topic for her American audience. Soon *Harper's Bazaar* and *Scribner's Magazine*, two of the most popular magazines in the United States, were purchasing her stories as well.

One spring day in 1893, Tarbell found Samuel McClure waiting by the door of her Paris apartment. The publisher, who had recently founded *McClure's Magazine* in New York City, had seen Tarbell's work and wanted the talented writer on his staff.

Her first assignment for McClure was a series of interviews with France's leading female writers. Although Tarbell met with successful editors, journalists, and novelists, she concluded that no woman had yet produced "authentic biographical, historical or scientific articles." She felt the successful writer would possess "the power to grasp immediately the salient features of a subject . . . and to add to it facts, comparisons, [and] opinions" to help others understand the topic. The woman who could do that, she concluded, would "win appreciation and position long before she has to go a-begging."

Tarbell intended to become that woman writer. She soon proved she could explain scientific details to readers as clearly as she had the culture and people of Paris.

Assigned by McClure to interview the great French scientist Louis Pasteur, Tarbell wrote her piece with such clarity that McClure pleaded with her to join him at the magazine's headquarters in New York City. In 1894, Tarbell finally agreed to return to the United States.

One of the most celebrated scientists of the era, Louis Pasteur (1822-1895) had developed a vaccine for the dreaded rabies in 1885. Three years later, he founded the Pasteur Institute for disease research in Paris.

While Tarbell was steadily gaining popularity in America with her features from Paris, John Rockefeller continued to crush his competition for oil revenue. His conquest of the oil industry had been largely finished by 1880, at which time Standard Oil refined 95 percent of the oil drilled in the United States. By 1882, he had formed the Standard Oil Trust, a group of 40 corporations throughout the industry, giving the tycoon nearly total control over American oil production. He was well on his way to becoming America's first billionaire in 1894.

Over the next five years, Tarbell built up the experience that would make it possible to take on Standard Oil. Two major serial biographies she wrote made her a household name. Her first subject was Napoleon Bonaparte, the military general who had led France to the height of European power before his defeat in 1815. The other figure was Abraham Lincoln, whose assassination in 1865 had stunned a nation already shaken from four years of the bloody Civil War.

Just before Tarbell's account of Bonaparte appeared in the November 1894 issue of *McClure's*, the magazine's circulation stood at 24,500. Overnight, readership soared to 65,000. Newspapers around the country praised the work. Tarbell's story was "the best short life of Napoleon we have ever seen," cried the *New York Press*, while the *Boston Globe* lauded the author's "painstaking research." By the time the serial ended in April 1895, circulation had climbed to 100,000 copies per issue.

Tarbell's popularity shot still higher with the debut of "The Life of Abraham Lincoln" in November 1895.

Tarbell felt that Napoleon Bonaparte (1769-1821) was "the greatest genius of his time," but that he "lacked the crown of greatness."

By year's end, *McClure's* passed the 250,000 mark in circulation. The Lincoln biography was so popular that McClure was unable to print enough magazines to keep pace with demand. When the series ended in September 1899, Tarbell was ready to face her biggest challenge— Standard Oil's John D. Rockefeller.

The muckraking movement Tarbell soon joined was a reaction to decades of unchecked political and business corruption. The United States had seen enormous economic growth after the end of the Civil War in 1865. Giants like Standard Oil swallowed whole industries while federal and local governments turned a blind eye to the special economic privileges—like the drastically reduced transportation rates enjoyed by Standard—that huge companies had the power to demand.

The staff of *McClure's* wanted to focus attention on a single *trust*, or monopoly, in order to illustrate how all monopolies operated. When Tarbell recounted how her father had initially profited in the oil business, only to be wiped out by the massive Standard, McClure was intrigued. He approved a three-part series targeting Rockefeller's trust. Despite warnings from her father that Rockefeller "will ruin the magazine," Tarbell immediately went to work investigating Standard Oil.

Rockefeller's operation had already been scrutinized by congressional committees in 1872 and 1876. In 1879, the states of New York, Ohio, and Pennsylvania had also launched investigations. Tarbell examined the results of these largely ineffective probes. While some documents had been destroyed, apparently at Standard's request, the muckraker unearthed one document that proved Rockefeller had indeed used illegal and monopolistic methods. Armed with this information, Tarbell began "The History of the Standard Oil Company."

In the December 1902 issue of *McClure's Magazine*, Tarbell described "a dozen or more small oil refineries"

"Whenever a man succeeds remarkably in any particular line of business," complained John D. Rockefeller (1839-1937), *"socialists and anarchists"* like Tarbell *"jump on him and cry him down."*

that had been "strung along the banks of Walworth and Kingsbury" near Cleveland, Ohio, in the early 1860s. She then revealed how by 1878 Standard had steadily gobbled up the small oil producers in the area to form a mammoth company that controlled almost all of the oil production in the United States by the turn of the century. For the next two years, the meticulous muckraker hammered away at Standard Oil in the pages of *McClure's*.

Tarbell's articles were a sensation. On the strength of her serial, and two other exposés by *McClure's* staffers Lincoln Steffens and Ray Stannard Baker, Sam McClure's publication became the most popular reform-minded magazine in the country. For the next nine years, nearly 2,000 muckraking articles were published in American magazines. According to one historian, "close to a third were written by a small group of 12 men and one woman who concentrated on and professionalized this kind of journalism." That one woman was Ida Tarbell. In the words of McClure, she had become "the most generally famous woman in America."

Following magazine publication, in 1904 the Standard Oil series was released under the same title as a book that one critic called "the most remarkable book of its kind ever written in this country." Whatever his concerns about muckraking in general, President Roosevelt obviously agreed with Tarbell's conclusions. In November 1906, the federal government took Standard Oil to court, charging the monopoly with obstructing interstate trade, a violation of the 1890 Sherman Antitrust Act. Standard had interfered with trade, the government argued, by destroying most of its competition and seizing control of the nation's oil market. When the court ruled against Standard, the oil giant appealed, but in May 1911 the U.S. Supreme Court upheld the ruling. Rockefeller was forced to break up the Standard Oil Trust.

But that was only one reform Tarbell's muckraking helped to enact. At the root of Standard's power was its control of the transportation systems that enabled it to ship oil at a rate far below that offered to its shrinking competition. The 1906 Hepburn Act provided for tighter government control of railroad rates. Four years later, the Mann-Elkins Act allowed Washington to regulate oil pipeline rates. Finally, in 1914, the Clayton Act outlawed unfair competition that could lead to monopolies.

94

In 1906, while Standard struggled in the courts, Tarbell moved on to other subjects—and to a different magazine. She left *McClure's* after Sam McClure, having gained fame and fortune attacking trusts, decided to form his own financial empire. The publisher planned a McClure's School Book Company and even a McClure's Bank. Tarbell was disillusioned by her boss's greed. With other *McClure's* staff members, she founded a new journal, the *American Magazine.*

At the *American*, Tarbell continued to chronicle the history of big business in hopes of bringing about reform. One of her popular themes was the tariff on imported or exported goods that was meant to protect certain industries from competition. In a series that ran for two years following its December 1906 debut, Tarbell focused the tariff question on the single issue most important to her readers—Did tariffs harm American consumers by making them pay more for basic goods?

Tarbell's detailed research of congressional records, interviews, and books showed that while the nation's wealth was increasing as never before, "a vast number of hard-working people in this country are really having a more difficult time making ends meet." For example, shoemakers had to pay more for their materials because of a tariff designed to protect the leather industry. In order to make profits, the cobblers passed on their increased cost to the consumers of shoes. Public indignation sparked partly by Tarbell's articles forced Congress to pass the Payne-Aldrich Tariff Act in August 1909, which gave the president authority to set maximum tariff rates.

Although best known for business investigations, Tarbell addressed other subjects as well, including the women's rights movement. Her views on women's issues had changed considerably through the years. In her 1912 book, *The Business of Being a Woman*, Tarbell argued, "The central fact of women's life—Nature's reason for her—is the child, his bearing and rearing." Feminists gasped as America's most famous working woman added: "There is no escape from the divine order that [a woman's] life must be built around this constraint." In the family, as in the business world, people must meet their obligations.

Activists like these women marching for voting rights in 1917 were appalled that Tarbell would advise women not to follow their career dreams as she had.

In 1915, Tarbell finally left the *American* to devote her energies once again to freelance writing. An expert on labor relations, she also appeared before the Federal Commission on Industrial Relations in January 1915. A year later, President Woodrow Wilson invited Tarbell to become the first woman to sit on his Tariff Commission. Believing the commission stood little chance of affecting legislation in a Congress controlled by powerful business interests, Tarbell declined the president's offer. But she did serve on several other government and labor committees over the next few years.

A highlight of Tarbell's later career came in 1925, when *McCall's Magazine* asked her to travel to Italy to interview the country's Fascist dictator, Benito Mussolini. The subsequent series was generally favorable to the leader. Tarbell described the improved productivity and efficiency of Italy and the housing Mussolini had built for workers. She did caution, however, that the dictator's autocratic style could lead him to abuse his power.

Indeed, Mussolini was already cooperating with Adolf Hitler in his designs on Europe when Tarbell published her autobiography, *All in a Day's Work*, in 1939. This book was her last major work. On January 6, 1944, Ida Tarbell died of pneumonia at the age of 86. Even if her views of Mussolini were misguided and her attitudes towards careers for women were inconsistent, Tarbell is honored as one of the first muckrakers and as the journalist who challenged the mighty Standard Oil Company.

Alfred Harmsworth (1865-1922), who controlled the largest group of periodicals in the world in addition to his newspaper holdings, bragged that his publishing empire was based on trivia.

6

Alfred Harmsworth
Napoleon of Fleet Street

*B*ritish publisher Alfred Harmsworth once tried on a hat that had been owned by Napoleon Bonaparte. "It fits me," he noted with satisfaction. He was also pleased when a waiter in Paris told him he looked just like the legendary French emperor. Napoleon had been a daring general and empire-builder—precisely the kind of role model Harmsworth admired. Indeed, for nearly 30 years the publisher ruled Fleet Street—where the London press is based—as surely as Napoleon ever ruled his empire.

Harmsworth, whom historians often call the founder of the modern British newspaper, broke new ground in print journalism. By catering to the tastes of a newly literate public in the late 1800s, Harmsworth pioneered the popular mass-market press. Think of him when you read articles about whether women need love more than men or why broccoli is good for your health.

Harmsworth's newspapers, like those of William Randolph Hearst in the United States, also fed—and helped to create—the public's desire for exciting stories about crime, corruption, and threats to national security. And, like his American counterpart, Harmsworth had the ability to package his product to appeal to the greatest number of readers.

Alfred Charles Harmsworth was born on July 15, 1865, in Chapelizod, a village outside Dublin, Ireland. When Alfred was a child, his family moved to London, where his father, who was slipping into alcoholism, struggled to make ends meet with an unsuccessful law practice.

Because young Harmsworth loved nothing more than quietly reading horror stories called "penny dreadfuls," he did poorly in school. Worse, he was interested in journalism, a career his father—like many educated middle-class people of the time—considered vulgar. At age 13, Alfred was already editor of his school's magazine.

Alfred was full of get-rich-quick schemes—like the medicine made from soap he once cooked up in his family's kitchen. He believed there was money to be made in magazines and newspapers. Education had become compulsory in England in 1880, so more people than ever before were able to read. These new readers wanted something more interesting than stodgy articles about

British politics. New publications were popping up that offered short humorous pieces or stories about crime that appealed to a mass readership.

By 1883, the teenager was contributing articles to several of these periodicals, and he soon became editor of a short-lived magazine called *Youth*. Three years later, Harmsworth was making a living writing for *Tit-Bits*, a widely read magazine of fascinating trivia. Even then the 21-year-old was planning a rival magazine. But he needed cash. In 1886, Harmsworth showed his potential to likely investors when he revamped *Bicycling News* to make it a stylish magazine.

Within two years, the budding publisher had located an investor for the magazine he envisioned. *Answers to Correspondents* was designed as responses to questions— any questions—sent in by readers (although in actuality Harmsworth wrote most of the questions too). Now the British public could read "What the Queen Eats" and articles about what it felt like to be hanged. While some in-depth responses reported on subjects like life behind bars in London's prisons, most dealt with useless information like "how madmen write" or "horseflesh as food." Readers flocked to newsstands to chuckle as Harmsworth and his staff tried to answer any off-the-wall query.

Harmsworth worked creatively to make *Answers* profitable. When he devised a contest offering a British pound a week for life—then enough money to live on—250,000 readers bought the issue announcing the winner. To attract advertisers' revenue to the paper, Harmsworth ran a number of articles about advertising and business. Within a year, the magazine sold close to 50,000 copies per issue and was turning a small profit.

Slowly, as Alfred's younger brothers joined the business, Harmsworth's publishing empire began to take shape. In 1890, Alfred and his brother Harold, whose aptitude for finance and marketing complemented Alfred's talent for editing, launched a series of inexpensive magazines for general readers. Some of the most popular titles eventually included *Comic Cuts*, which was stuffed with jokes as well as trivia; *Funny Wonder*, a compilation of humorous illustrations; and *Forget-me-Not*, a wildly successful women's magazine.

Harmsworth's plan—which he called his "Schemo Magnifico"—was to flood the market with popular, half-penny magazines. Bringing them out at an average of one every six months, he would drive the competition, priced at a penny, out of business. By the end of 1892, the brothers were reaping huge profits as their most successful publications sold over a million and a half copies weekly.

Not yet 29, Alfred began to live the life of a country gentleman with his wife, Mary, whom he had married in 1888. Authors visited his home and spent afternoons fishing or playing tennis as they discussed story ideas. Alfred's brothers or his staff ran the office in his absence.

In *Halfpenny Marvel, Union Jack*, and *Pluck Library*— which were all up and running by late 1894—Alfred began publishing adventure tales, where swashbuckling heroes rescued damsels in distress and conquered exotic lands. He advertised these magazines as uplifting fiction for boys who were in danger of being corrupted by the penny dreadfuls he himself had devoured. One of his authors was Arthur Conan Doyle, who had begun writing his Sherlock Holmes stories just a few years before.

In the summer of 1894, Alfred and Harold got into newspaper publishing when they purchased and revitalized the nearly bankrupt *Evening News and Post*. Up to this time, few British papers modeled themselves after their flashier American cousins, but Alfred Harmsworth was determined to change all that. He shortened stories and enlarged headlines while increasing coverage of sports and crime. In September, the *Evening News* began a series on a murderer waiting to be hanged. The public was fascinated. By December, when the man was executed, sales had jumped from 180,000 to 313,000 copies.

Sir Arthur Conan Doyle (1859-1930) created his first Sherlock Holmes detective story in 1887. Unlike the daring heroes of adventure tales, Holmes saved the day through his shrewd intelligence.

The hallmark of the paper, however, was to be its intense British patriotism and paranoia about foreign attacks on the British Empire. At the time, the British were beginning to feel threatened by the emerging German nation under the brash young Kaiser Wilhelm II. Harmsworth hammered away at the perceived German menace. The kaiser was a "hotblooded and eccentric" leader, blared the *Evening News*, whose desire for an empire of his own was a danger to the British people.

Early in 1896, Alfred decided to establish a new daily paper. He promoted its debut as "the busy man's paper," but even he was amazed when the *Daily Mail* set a

The grandson of Great Britain's Queen Victoria, Kaiser Wilhelm II (1859-1941) was only 29 when he became ruler of the German empire.

new world's record by selling nearly 400,000 copies on its first day of publication. "We've struck a gold mine!" Harmsworth exclaimed to a colleague that landmark day.

Staffed by experts, the *Daily Mail* was Harmsworth's greatest achievement. What Alfred created was the modern newspaper, complete with wire-service reports from around the world, lengthy coverage of sports and business, human-interest stories, and feature articles on hot topics—all with a patriotic tone. Many of its features are commonplace in today's newsrooms, but at the time they represented true innovations in the British press. And unlike other British dailies, Harmsworth's paper was not the mouthpiece of a political party. As with his magazines, Harmsworth halved the going price for a paper, selling "the penny newspaper for one halfpenny."

In addition to stories arriving by wire and telephone, Harmsworth sent foreign correspondents to cover the growing British conflict in South Africa with the Dutch descendants who were, he noted, armed by the Germans. War eventually erupted in October 1899. Well-written stories, accompanied by maps and diagrams, gave the *Daily Mail* the best international coverage of any British paper. Harmsworth's investment was rewarded with a daily readership that sometimes topped 1 million.

Ever attentive to his readers, Harmsworth printed stories about the weather and holidays, subjects not deemed "newsworthy" by other papers. Many feature articles were designed to appeal to women, who had been largely ignored by other dailies. He also published articles about marriage and relations between the sexes sure to arouse controversy in conservative England. If readers failed to send in comments about the topics, Harmsworth and his staff wrote fake letters.

Harmsworth hoped to establish a newspaper monopoly in Great Britain that would bring journalism "to a standard of excellence hitherto unattained." His idea of excellence—like Hearst's in the United States— was not absolute accuracy. The *Daily Mail* "may not always be entirely truthful," conceded Harmsworth, "but it is always interesting and always on the spot." With his patriotic stories that defended the British Empire, Harmsworth believed his paper expressed the voice of the people. But he also used his power to shape public opinion, attacking politicians whose views differed from his own anti-German nationalistic obsessions.

With the success of the *Daily Mail*, Alfred soon rubbed elbows with celebrities and leading politicians. In 1904, the British government honored Harmsworth for his contributions to journalism by naming him a *baronet*, an honorary British title directly above a knight. Less than 18 months later, he received the higher title of baron, making him Alfred, Lord Northcliffe.

While Harmsworth had a knack for predicting what the public wanted, his career was not without failure. In 1903, he launched the *Daily Mirror*. He promoted it as "the first daily newspaper for gentlewomen" and hired a news staff consisting mostly of women reporters and editors. Having pioneered the women's magazine market with *Forget-me-Not* in the 1890s, Harmsworth had good reason to count on the *Daily Mirror*'s success.

Although the first issue of the *Mirror* sold 265,000 copies, daily circulation fell below 100,000 copies during the second week of publication and continued to plummet. The paper's attempt to publish both international news and articles about cooking and entertainment made it a hodgepodge that had little appeal. Harmsworth fired the female staff and revamped the *Daily Mirror*, using new (and not very successful) techniques to print photographs. By the time these changes and a cut-rate price increased sales, however, Harmsworth had lost interest in the newspaper. He eventually sold his share to his brother Harold.

Like Hearst in the United States, Harmsworth purchased additional papers as he gained greater success. In 1901, Alfred and Harold had formed Amalgamated Press to run their dozens of magazines. Now, in 1905, Alfred founded Associated Newspapers to manage his growing newspaper empire. He owned a number of city and regional newspapers in addition to the *Mail*, *Mirror*, and *Evening News*, with a total circulation in excess of 2 million. When he purchased the prestigious but struggling *Times* of London in 1908, Harmsworth had become the Napoleon of Fleet Street.

At times, Harmsworth abused his power to reach the public. Sometimes he suppressed stories to protect his friends. More often, he got into trouble for what he *did* print. In October 1906, the *Mail* published articles about the Lever Brothers Soap Company's decision to decrease the size of its three-penny soap, as well as the company's plans to kill the competition by forming a soap trust.

Editorial cartoons in the *Mirror* portrayed Lever executives as thieves picking the pockets of consumers.

Although Lever was forming a soap trust and had cut the weight of its soap, Harmsworth's attacks were reckless. Worried he would lose advertising from other soap companies and sure the public would be enraged at Lever, Harmsworth made little effort to distinguish between fact and opinion in his papers' coverage.

When Lever's sales began to plummet, the company fought back with a libel suit against Harmsworth, seeking compensation for lost sales and business deals. The *Mail* had published a story about a poor woman who took in laundry to feed her children. She could not afford to buy the extra soap, and her children were going hungry. Because the story was fictitious, Lever won the lawsuit. Harmsworth was forced to pay Lever and the other companies involved 151,000 British pounds.

Business corruption was only one of Harmsworth's obsessions. A more lasting preoccupation—dating back to the mid-1890s—remained the German threat. Great Britain had long depended on its navy to maintain its overseas possessions, but Kaiser Wilhelm was determined to build Germany a powerful fleet to challenge the British. Harmsworth watched in horror as the two countries rushed to build *dreadnoughts*, powerful battleships that outclassed all previous models. His fears were realized when the First World War began in 1914.

As people picked up the *Daily Mail* to read about the war's progress, Harmsworth railed against the British government for not adequately supporting its soldiers. He conducted a campaign for a draft and complained about wartime censorship of the press.

On May 21, 1915, Harmsworth wrote a long article entitled "The Tragedy of the Shells." In the article, he charged that a shortage of ammunition was destroying the British army. When the government of Herbert Henry Asquith collapsed in December 1916 as a result of widespread dissatisfaction with its wartime leadership, Harmsworth congratulated himself for bringing the government down. Aware of his awesome power, he told one colleague, "I believe the independent newspaper to be one of the future forms of government."

Harmsworth's magnified sense of his own importance was becoming dangerous as well as embarrassing. To keep him under control, the new prime minister,

William Maxwell Aitken, Lord Beaverbrook, (1879-1964), who purchased the first of his several papers in 1916, eventually surpassed Harmsworth as a politically powerful newspaper magnate in England.

David Lloyd George, asked Harmsworth to lead a mission to the United States in 1917. After his return in 1918, the government found Harmsworth a position well suited to his skills and obsessions. Early in the war, he had suggested dropping leaflets over Germany to weaken its resolve to fight. Now, as the new director of war propaganda, Harmsworth was able to implement his tactic.

But Harmsworth also wanted a greater role in the government. With the war's end in sight in autumn 1918, he hoped for a role in the peace negotiations. Prime Minister David Lloyd George refused the publisher.

David Lloyd George (second from left) meets with world leaders Vittorio Emanuele Orlando, premier of Italy (left); French premier Georges Clemenceau (second from right); and U.S. President Woodrow Wilson (right) after the end of World War I.

Furious, Harmsworth used his papers to try to ruin the popular British leader for being soft on the Germans.

Harmsworth had long suffered from poor health and a volatile temperament. During World War I, his behavior worsened. His rages at employees and friends over petty disagreements became more frequent as both his paranoia and his grandiose ideas of his own power and importance swelled.

In 1921, at the age of 56, Harmsworth finally retired for the sake of his health. Mentally unstable and suffering a host of physical ailments, he nevertheless set off on a trip around the world with his wife. Even then, he sent cables ordering his managers to cut the price of the *Times* to increase readership or to run a particular story about the conflicts in Ireland. A year later, Harmsworth's condition deteriorated into insanity. He imagined plots to kill him and sent bizarre threatening telegrams to his editors. After suffering from delirium for two months, 57-year-old Alfred Harmsworth died on August 14, 1922.

Harmsworth's newspapers gradually strayed from the family. Although Harold Harmsworth reorganized the family's holdings as the Daily Mail Trust, he sold the *Times* in 1922 and the *Mirror* in 1931. By 1932, when Harold dissolved Northcliffe Newspapers into the parent company of Associated Newspapers, the Harmsworths were mostly out of the business. But the papers have survived. Today, the innovative *Daily Mail* remains a giant in the newspaper industry, with daily sales of over 1.6 million. The *Daily Mirror* sells even better—an astounding 2.6 million papers every day.

Knowing the potential of television, Edward R. Murrow (1908-1965) warned, "We shall pay for using this most powerful instrument of communication to insulate the citizenry from the hard and demanding realities which must be faced if we are to survive."

112

7

Edward R. Murrow
A Voice You Could Trust

*E*ven though Ed Murrow pioneered news broadcasting on both radio and television, he did not find these inventions crucial to reporting. "They will broadcast truth or falsehood with equal facility," he told his staff in January 1964, the day he retired as director of the United States Information Agency (USIA). With political intrigue at home and turmoil abroad, truth was the most important element of journalism, whatever the medium. Above all, people needed a voice they could trust.

No one was in a better position to talk about broadcasting than Murrow. He had made his radio debut in

1930, when the first commercial radio station in the country—KDKA in Pittsburgh, Pennsylvania—was only 10 years old. Because of his ability, radio would grow into the most popular source for news. Then, when television shot to stardom in the late 1940s, viewers again tuned in to Murrow's broadcasts. Simply put, people trusted Ed Murrow.

Egbert Roscoe Murrow was born in Greensboro, North Carolina, on April 25, 1908. He was the youngest of Roscoe and Ethel's three surviving sons. When "Egg" was four years old, the Murrows moved to Blanchard, Washington, to farm. The farming operation was not successful, but when Roscoe found work as an engineer on a logging train, the family's financial situation improved.

While maintaining an excellent record at Edison High School, Egg began cutting timber to bring in money. He also played on the school's championship basketball team, represented his classmates in the student government, and starred on the debating team.

After graduating at the top of his high-school class, 18-year-old Edward—he changed his name from the hated "Egbert" around this time—entered Washington State College in 1926. There he acted in plays, served in the campus Reserve Officers' Training Corps, won election as class president, and again shone on the school's debate team. By the time he graduated in 1930, Murrow had grown accustomed to success and leadership.

Two weeks after graduating, Murrow was on his way to New York City to begin a one-year term as the newly elected president of the National Student Federation of

America (NSFA). His primary task in the NSFA, a group founded five years earlier to spread knowledge and understanding among the world's students, was to organize overseas tours for American and international students.

The unpaid position offered valuable opportunities. For instance, Murrow traveled throughout Europe for eight weeks, gaining insight into European politics and culture. In addition, he hosted a weekly radio series on the two-year-old Columbia Broadcasting System (CBS).

On the CBS series, *The University of the Air*, international leaders addressed students around the world. Murrow arranged broadcasts of interviews with Mahatma Gandhi—whose nonviolent movement would pressure Britain to grant independence to India in 1947—as well as with British prime minister Ramsay MacDonald and German president Paul von Hindenburg. By 1931, Murrow was running the show.

In December 1931, Murrow became assistant director of the Institute of International Education (IIE), an organization formed in 1919 to promote peace through the international exchange of ideas and knowledge. Murrow's main task was to recruit well-known scholars from Europe to lecture in the United States.

By May 1933, two months after Germany's population had elected Adolf Hitler their new leader, Murrow was involved in relocating to the United States German scholars facing persecution by Hitler's Nazi officials. Within two years, the young assistant director was practically running the IIE and rubbing elbows with some of the world's greatest scientists and educators.

Murrow loved his job, except for one problem—his boss had no intention of quitting or allowing his assistant to take over. Realizing he would never be promoted, in September 1935 Murrow accepted a position with the CBS radio network to coordinate overseas transmissions dealing with foreign affairs. It was a risky move for Murrow because radio was still little known as a source of international stories. But in December 1936, the new director of overseas transmissions changed all that.

Earlier in 1936, King Edward VIII of England had announced his desire to marry a soon-to-be-divorced American woman. As the situation exploded into a major crisis for the British government, Murrow organized thorough radio coverage. On December 11, CBS scooped the newspapers by being the first to report that Edward was *abdicating*, or giving up his crown. It was a tremendous victory for the broadcast medium, confirming that newspapers could never report a story as quickly as radio. Suddenly, Ed Murrow was a star at CBS.

Six months later, as political tensions between Germany and the rest of Europe escalated, Murrow was named European director for CBS. He was asked to organize the network's overseas broadcasting in case of war. What the new director found upon his arrival in London in May 1937 was a shoestring operation housed in a single office. Nonetheless, he set to work, intent on making CBS the world leader in overseas broadcasting.

The network faced a major test in March 1938. In a maneuver known as the *Anschluss*—German for "joining"—Nazi forces invaded the ethnically German country

Adolf Hitler (1889-1945) was cheered by crowds of patriotic Germans seduced by his vision of a new and powerful German empire.

of Austria, determined to force all Germans to live together in one country. As Hitler's army approached the Austrian capital of Vienna, the National Broadcasting Company (NBC) was beating CBS by transmitting eye-witness accounts of the invasion. Murrow was desperately searching for some way to gain the edge when one of his staff members suggested something never before tried: CBS could report reactions from five major European capitals—London, Paris, Berlin, Rome, and Vienna—together on the same show.

Despite their inexperience, Murrow's staff per-formed nearly flawlessly. The broadcast was another milestone for radio—the new medium could deliver the news instantly from all over the world.

Six months after the *Anschluss*, Hitler pressed the Czechoslovakian government to hand over a part of their country populated mostly by Germans. As war threatened, both CBS and NBC broadcast nonstop. In fact, people living in the United States were better informed about the war than many Europeans.

During the summer-long crisis, millions of listeners tuned their radios to hear Murrow. According to one magazine critic, the CBS reporter exerted "more influence upon America's reaction to foreign news than a shipful of newspapermen." Murrow fully understood the awesome responsibility of a radio journalist. As he had told his colleagues a year earlier, networks must always "seek for truth wherever it might be found" and spread "that truth as widely as possible."

In the end, there was no war in 1938. Britain and France gave Adolf Hitler everything he wanted in Czechoslovakia—without even consulting the Czechs! But when Poland refused a similar territorial demand in 1939, Hitler launched a *Blitzkrieg*—or "lightning war"— to take Poland by force. Two days later, on September 3, Britain and France finally declared war.

Murrow transmitted weekly reports of the war from London. Hitler quickly trounced Poland and then turned on France on May 10, 1940. Five weeks later, German troops were entering Paris in triumph.

On September 7, Nazi pilots flying out of captured French airfields began bombing London. From the roof of the CBS building, Murrow described for listeners how waves of German bombers had demolished large sections

"The scale of this air war is so great that the reporting of it is not easy," Murrow broadcast from London in September 1940. He wandered the city looking for damage to describe and people to interview for his listeners back home.

of London in just a few hours. Within weeks, millions of Americans were eating their evening meals by the radio, engrossed in Murrow's eyewitness accounts of the Battle of Britain. Even newspapers began printing his reports as columns, all but admitting what the public already knew— Ed Murrow had become the dominant source for news.

Besides revolutionizing news reporting, Murrow was trying to change the course of almost two centuries of American foreign policy. With the exception of entering World War I in 1917, the United States had all but ignored the affairs of Europe. Now, even with Nazi bombers obliterating London, most Americans still hoped to maintain their policy of isolation. As Murrow told

British listeners, he hoped his broadcasts would force people in the United States to think "for the first time of America's responsibility as a nation."

On December 7, 1941, the U.S. fleet docked at Pearl Harbor, Hawaii, was nearly destroyed by a Japanese sneak attack. Four days later, Germany and Italy declared war on the United States. America now had no choice but to fight the Axis powers of Japan, Germany, and Italy. The war in Europe had raged for over two years by the time of America's entry, and Murrow growled in disgust that the U.S. did not enter the war willingly—"it was *bombed* into it at Pearl Harbor."

In their bombing of Pearl Harbor, the Japanese destroyed 19 ships and 188 aircraft. A total of 2,280 soldiers and sailors were killed, and 1,109 more were wounded.

By the end of 1942, the Allies—Britain, the Soviet Union, and the United States—began to wear down the Germans in Europe. While the Soviets battled the Nazis in the east, on November 8, 1942, American troops landed on Germany's southern flank in North Africa. On June 6, 1944—D-Day—Allied forces under General Dwight D. Eisenhower invaded the beaches of northern France. Hitler's forces were finally on the retreat.

As the Germans wilted in the face of superior force, the reputation of Ed Murrow and "Murrow's Boys" grew. By late 1943, he had assembled what one journalist called "the finest news staff anybody had ever put together in Europe." Murrow's secret was to hire people who "knew what they were talking about . . . even though they might not win any elocution [public speaking] contests." That meant hiring newspaper reporters in addition to veterans of radio. Truth and accuracy, not entertainment, was Murrow's chief goal.

By the end of August 1945, the Axis powers had surrendered unconditionally. On Christmas Day, CBS promoted Murrow to vice-president and director of public affairs. Now he controlled the network's worldwide corps of news reporters.

One of Murrow's new projects was a series of monthly documentaries that focused on American social issues such as poverty and juvenile crime. The first show, a nationwide tour of ghettos and death rows, was a hit. "CBS has demonstrated," praised *Time* magazine, "that when radio has something to say about an important problem—and says it intelligently—people will listen."

Despite his success, Murrow was never happy as an executive. He resigned his position in July 1947 to resume his beloved broadcasting duties.

Murrow launched a radio series called *Hear It Now* in December 1950, but his attention was more and more drawn to the fledgling medium that he believed would soon be the new king of broadcasting—television. Back in 1934, inventor Philo Farnsworth had been the first to publicly demonstrate the electronic television. The advent of World War II had interrupted the establishment of the new medium as electronics factories shifted to the production of war supplies. When televisions were produced after the war, however, viewership steadily rose. Having recognized television's potential as early as 1939, Murrow now initiated a television series for CBS called *See It Now*.

In typical Murrow fashion, the first half-hour show on November 18, 1951, made history. To demonstrate television's ability, the camera showed Murrow looking into two television monitors, one broadcasting live from San Francisco, California, the other transmitting a live shot from New York City. It was the first time that residents from both the East and West Coasts could see each other at the same time.

Thirteen months later, on December 28, 1952, the broadcaster scored again with "Christmas in Korea," a report from the war there that the *New York Times* called "one of the finest programs ever seen on TV." Gone were the romantic newsreel images and sanitized battle reports from Washington that had characterized previous wartime newscasts. Based on weeks of interviews, this show portrayed the confusion and frustration felt by the average soldier. Impressed by the most realistic war footage ever broadcast, viewers knew they were seeing the truth. They came to trust Murrow as never before.

It was a good thing they did. In early 1954, Murrow used his program to confront Senator Joseph McCarthy, the powerful leader of the reckless anti-Communist movement now known as *McCarthyism*. The Wisconsin senator had spent the previous four years stamping many officials in the United States government as Soviet-backed traitors. Because of McCarthy's hype, anti-Communist hysteria gripped the nation. Murrow knew that only

In 1952, Joseph McCarthy (1908-1957) had claimed, "I have here in my hand a list of 205 names" of Communists in the State Department. But he never offered proof of his allegations.

someone with his reputation as a trusted voice could stand up to the senator.

On March 9, the host of *See It Now* devoted the entire program to refuting McCarthy's charges. "We must remember always," Murrow told his audience, "that accusation is not proof and that conviction depends upon evidence and due process of law." He then showed that most of the senator's accusations were either half-truths or flat-out lies.

It was Murrow's greatest moment in broadcasting and the beginning of a rapid fall for McCarthy. In August, 51 percent of respondents to a Gallup opinion poll opposed McCarthy, up from just 29 percent in January. In December, just nine months after Murrow's exposé, the Senate voted to condemn McCarthy for his witch-hunt tactics. Murrow had become, in the words of one magazine article, "practically . . . a national hero."

As the 1950s progressed, Murrow continued to be broadcasting's biggest star. A new series, *Person to Person*, in which Murrow interviewed celebrities, made him popular with an increasing number of viewers who watched television for entertainment only. It was not the kind of program the newsman enjoyed hosting, but CBS gave Murrow no choice. Television networks were earning more and more money from corporate advertising, with widely popular shows like *Person to Person* taking in far more revenue than less-watched news broadcasts like *See It Now*. Disturbed, Murrow warned that corporations could alter—and even cause the cancellation of—shows simply by withholding their advertising dollars.

CBS justified his fears in March 1958 by canceling *See It Now*. Murrow was disgusted that profit margins should control the flow of information. "There is a great and perhaps decisive battle to be fought against ignorance, intolerance, and indifference," he contended. "This weapon of television could be useful."

Despite reduction of airtime, polls still proclaimed Murrow the public's favorite news commentator. But all was not well. Already depressed over the commercialization of television, Murrow also began to experience health problems—doubtless as a result of smoking four packs of cigarettes a day. He would suddenly appear trembling or flushed and, in early 1959, he was even forced by illness to bow out of a newscast only moments before airtime. Needing a break, Murrow began a year-long sabbatical in July.

Soon after his return to CBS in the summer of 1960, the network canceled *Small World*, Murrow's last remaining show, for lack of sponsorship. Although still popular with viewers, Murrow was disliked by sponsors because his hard-hitting reports were controversial. Advertisers generally tried to avoid controversy. Also, with Walter Cronkite and Eric Sevareid, CBS no longer had a shortage of talented news commentators. As the odd man out, Murrow dangled uselessly.

In January 1961, Ed Murrow left broadcasting for good. The new president of the United States, John F. Kennedy, had selected him to direct the United States Information Agency (USIA). Murrow's responsibility was the overseas promotion of U.S. foreign policy.

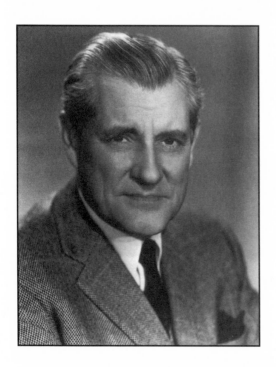

One of "Murrow's Boys" in the World War II broadcasts, Eric Sevareid went on to become one of the United States' most respected television news correspondents.

He attacked the job with characteristic enthusiasm, often working 14-hour days. As always, accuracy and credibility were Murrow's main goals. "The measure of our success will be the degree to which we are believed," he told a Senate subcommittee, insisting that foreign listeners would easily see through slanted USIA newscasts.

But Murrow was no longer able to withstand the hectic pace he had kept at CBS. In October 1962, his health again failed. Although diagnosed with pneumonia, Murrow was soon back on the job. Doctors had discovered dark spots on his lungs, but they had explained them away as scar tissue from previous bouts with pneumonia.

A year later, the director was back in the hospital. The dark spots had grown; Murrow had lung cancer. In a three-hour operation, surgeons removed his left lung.

As Murrow recovered, President John F. Kennedy was assassinated in Dallas, Texas, on November 22, 1963, and Vice-President Lyndon B. Johnson became president. Never having liked Johnson, Murrow resigned two months later. In September 1964, Johnson nevertheless rewarded Murrow's lifelong achievement with the Medal of Freedom, America's highest civilian award.

By the end of the month, Murrow was again battling cancer; the disease had spread throughout his body. For six painful months, Murrow endured cancer treatments that caused him to lose his hair. On April 27, 1965, Ed Murrow died at the age of 57. The voice so many Americans had trusted was silenced far too early.

Lyndon B. Johnson (1908-1973) in August 1964. Murrow wrote to a friend that year, "The Johnson Administration is in the process of creating a real record of political opportunism."

Carl Bernstein (left) and Bob Woodward at the 1976 opening of All the President's Men, *the film based on their book about their investigation of Watergate*

8

Bob Woodward and Carl Bernstein
Watchdogs in Washington

*B*ob Woodward and Carl Bernstein were not fond of one another. Both in their late twenties and trying to work their way up at one of the United States' major newspapers, they could not have been more different. Woodward had a Yale degree and the military experience that in June 1972 marked him as a conservative. Bernstein was a long-haired college dropout who had a way with words. Together, however, the two reporters would become living legends. The series of investigative articles that Woodward and Bernstein wrote after a mysterious break-in at the Democratic headquarters at the Watergate building in Washington, D.C., would bring down a corrupt presidential administration.

Robert Upshur Woodward was born on March 26, 1943, in Geneva, Illinois, west of Chicago. Growing up in nearby Wheaton, Bob was active in sports, amateur radio, and school politics. His high-school yearbook named him "most likely to succeed."

To help pay his way through the prestigious Yale University in New Haven, Connecticut, Woodward enlisted in the Reserve Officers' Training Corps (ROTC) program and received a navy scholarship. Well liked, Woodward was on the staff of *Banner*, a group of Yale publications, and was chosen to join one of Yale's famous secret societies in his senior year.

As part of his scholarship, Woodward was required to serve in the U.S. Navy for four years after college. Three days after graduating with a degree in history and English, Ensign Woodward was assigned to be a circuit control officer aboard the U.S.S. *Wright*. This converted cruiser was a National Emergency Command Ship—a ship that the president or the Defense Department would use as a command base in the event of nuclear war. With top-secret security clearance, Woodward knew the codes for launching nuclear missiles.

In 1968, during the Vietnam War, Woodward oversaw the radio team and controlled the codes for the U.S.S. *Fox* off the coast of Vietnam. Lieutenant Woodward received the Navy Commendation Medal for his service the following year. Then the young naval officer went to Washington, D.C., to work for another year for the chief of naval operations in the Pentagon. His five-year stint in the navy and the Defense Department gave Woodward connections that would prove valuable in his future work.

In August 1970, one month after leaving the navy, Bob Woodward applied for a job with the *Washington Post*. He was so eager to get the job that he offered to work on an unpaid trial basis to prove himself.

Over the next three weeks, Woodward wrote 17 articles, but none of them was good enough for publication in the *Post*. Metropolitan editor Harry Rosenfeld thought Woodward had potential, however, and helped him find a position with the smaller *Montgomery County Sentinel* in nearby Rockville, Maryland. At the *Sentinel*, Woodward covered local and state news and wrote movie

Bob Woodward desperately wanted to be a reporter. At his interview for the Sentinel, *he told the editor, "I want to work here so bad I can taste it."*

reviews. He also wrote national stories. These articles, which he researched independently, were notable for their insider knowledge of Washington. Woodward's hard work paid off in September 1971, when Rosenfeld offered him a job at the *Post*. Just nine months later, he would begin his investigation of the Watergate break-in.

Carl Bernstein was born in Washington, D.C., on February 14, 1944, while his father was away at war. When Carl was 11, the Bernstein family moved to Silver Spring, Maryland, a suburb of Washington, D.C. Alfred Bernstein was a labor organizer and, like his wife, Sylvia, a Communist. As a boy, Carl was embarrassed by his parents' Communism and feared for their safety. He was mortified when the *Washington Post* published a photo of his mother being questioned about the Communist Party before a congressional committee.

Although his parents were atheists, Carl enrolled in a Hebrew course so he could have a *bar mitzvah*, a traditional coming-of-age ceremony for Jewish boys when they turn 13. During his early teens, he became the newsletter editor for a local branch of B'nai B'rith, a national Jewish youth organization.

Despite his active participation in B'nai B'rith and local television stardom as a dancer on a pop music show, Carl had trouble getting along with people and did poorly in school. He was suspended in eighth grade. In high school, he lost his driver's license for speeding and received a stiff fine for vandalizing the home of someone he claimed was anti-Semitic. Because he skipped so many classes to play pool, Carl nearly didn't graduate.

Recognizing that his son was not college material, Alfred Bernstein asked a friend of his to get 16-year-old Carl a job at the *Washington Evening Star*. There he worked as a *copy aide*—an entry-level position for people who want to break into newspaper reporting. The understaffed paper gave Bernstein the opportunity to write obituaries and later some articles. But the *Star* would not hire Bernstein as a full-time reporter because he did not have a college degree. Bernstein flunked out of the few classes he took at the University of Maryland because he wouldn't devote the time that was needed to do well.

In 1965, Bernstein left the *Star* for the *Elizabeth Daily Journal* in New Jersey. His feature story on the November 9, 1965, blackout in New York City won him

Carl Bernstein was thrilled to get a chance to advance in journalism. At the Elizabeth Daily Journal, *he wrote a column, "Of This and That," filled with eccentric people and unusual local events.*

a newswriting award, and the underqualified journalist suddenly was in demand. The following year, Bernstein accepted a reporting position with the *Washington Post*— the paper that had humiliated his family years before.

Bernstein did not fit in with the highly educated staff of the *Post*. But his colorful writing, extensive knowledge of his hometown, and uncanny ability to be where the story was gave him some success. He used techniques to wow readers by creating characters, scenes, and events as if he were writing a novel.

Yale alumnus Bob Woodward, who joined the staff five years after Bernstein, had more in common with the other reporters at the *Post* and was a favorite of executive editor Ben Bradlee. Soon his Yale connections, secret government contacts, and a good eye for scandal were getting him dozens of coveted page-one stories.

At first, the break-in at the national Democratic Party headquarters didn't seem like big news. The *Washington Post* assigned the story to the police beat, and eight reporters—including Woodward and Bernstein— spent the day investigating the unusual burglary. The June 18 article, under the byline of veteran police reporter Alfred Lewis, reported that five intruders, equipped with cameras and electronic bugs, had broken into the Democratic headquarters at the Watergate building. Their apparent leader was James McCord, a former CIA agent. Bernstein added a story identifying the other four men as anti-Communist Cuban activists from Miami.

On Monday, June 19, Woodward and Bernstein wrote their first story together. The article reported that

James McCord explains the bugging of the Watergate telephones at a later Senate hearing about the incident.

McCord was the security coordinator for the Committee to Re-elect the President (CRP), the group that was running Republican president Richard Nixon's reelection campaign. The two reporters continued to cover other news, but by August they were working exclusively on that story.

The *Post* had many more experienced reporters than Woodward and Bernstein. Most of them, however, were busy covering the presidential campaign or other major stories, so they had little time to spend looking into the burglary. And no one at the *Post* expected Watergate to turn into a groundbreaking story. In fact, few other newspapers in the nation were investigating Watergate.

The story began unfolding. On June 18, Woodward talked to a police source. Two of the burglars had the name "Howard E. Hunt" in their address books with "W. House" and "W. H." written next to his name. The next day, Woodward called the White House and learned that an E. Howard Hunt was a consultant for Charles Colson, the president's lawyer. Woodward then called Hunt at his public-relations firm and asked him why his name and phone number were in the burglars' address books. "Good God!" Hunt exclaimed. "In view that the matter is under adjudication, I have no comment." When Hunt slammed down the telephone, Woodward knew he was onto a big story.

E. Howard Hunt knew the extent of the cover-up of Watergate. To keep him quiet, White House officials gave him thousands of dollars. Hunt had also participated in other politically embarrassing and possibly illegal investigations of Democratic opponents and other Nixon enemies.

Woodward and Bernstein's first major breakthrough in the Watergate investigation came in late July. They got their lead from the *Post*'s top rival in Watergate coverage, the *New York Times*. The *Times* published an article detailing phone calls made by one of the burglars to CRP. Another *Times* story reported that a Mexican lawyer had placed $89,000 in a bank account of one of the arrested men. Why had the burglar called the Committee to Re-elect the President? Where had that $89,000 come from?

Bernstein used a contact he had at the phone company to obtain a record of the burglar's calls. Then he requested access to the burglar's phone and bank records from Florida state attorney Richard Gerstein. The reporter flew to Miami and finally horned his way in to talk to Gerstein's busy investigator. One of the checks on file was a $25,000 cashier's check made out to a Kenneth H. Dahlberg. Who was Kenneth Dahlberg and why was his check in the burglar's account?

Woodward would answer this question. Dahlberg, he learned, was a Minnesota businessman who was CRP's midwestern finance chair. Bewildered when Woodward asked him about the check, Dahlberg told the reporter he had given the $25,000 to CRP. The same check had wound up with one of the burglars!

Before their August 1 article that broke this story, Woodward and Bernstein had worked together grudgingly. After this story, however, all their articles carried their joint byline, and their editors at the *Post* began to refer to the duo as "Woodstein." Often, Woodward would write the first draft of an article and then Bernstein would rewrite it with more flare and drama. Their notes eventually filled four filing cabinets.

The reporters needed to find out who in CRP was involved with the burglary. Through a friend of another *Post* reporter, Woodward and Bernstein obtained a list of CRP employees. No one would answer questions on the telephone, so Woodward and Bernstein began visiting their homes at night. The CRP staffers were clearly scared of their superiors. "Please leave me alone," begged one, "you don't realize the pressure we're under." Others expressed fear that they were being watched. Go away, said one employee, "before they see you."

The CRP employees seemed most afraid of John Mitchell (left), the CRP director and former attorney general for President Richard Nixon (right).

Convinced they were onto something, Woodward and Bernstein tried another tactic. Using their hunches and bits of information they couldn't confirm, the two reporters acted like they knew more than they really did. Other CRP employees, they suggested to the nervous staff members, had named names. All they needed was confirmation. Slowly they began to identify top officials at CRP involved in the burglary and the cover-up.

Although Bernstein and Woodward were discovering more and more evidence of a conspiracy, just seven people were indicted for the Watergate incident on September 15, 1972. In addition to the five burglars, only E. Howard Hunt and G. Gordon Liddy, finance counsel to CRP, were named in the indictment. The FBI seemed satisfied that no one higher up knew about the burglary. White House officials then charged the *Post* with blowing the Watergate burglary out of proportion and giving it too much coverage.

But Woodward and Bernstein believed the break-in was not an isolated incident. Ever since June, Woodward had been receiving information from an old friend who was a White House official. This source gave Woodward information on the condition that it not be attributed to him. And Woodward would have to get confirmation of any information from another source before he could publish it. This official was providing the kind of confidential information journalists call "deep background," so one of the *Post* editors began jokingly referring to the source as "Deep Throat"—the title of a newly released pornographic film. The name stuck.

Deep Throat was risking his job by leaking information to the *Washington Post*. In their book about their investigation, Woodward and Bernstein wrote that when Woodward wanted to meet Deep Throat, he would put a red flag in a flowerpot on his apartment balcony. Then he would meet his friend at a prearranged time in an underground parking garage. When Deep Throat wanted to meet Woodward, he would draw a clock on page 20 of Woodward's *New York Times*. People have speculated about Deep Throat's identity ever since Woodward and Bernstein wrote *All the President's Men*.

Deep Throat hinted the full extent of the conspiracy. Woodward and Bernstein were able to confirm his allegations with former CRP treasurer Hugh Sloan Jr., as well as an anonymous FBI source and other sources. In a series of articles they wrote in October 1972, the reporters linked the Watergate break-in to a larger "dirty-tricks" campaign designed to ensure Richard Nixon's reelection. This secret campaign, which had been active during the Democratic primaries, was well organized and well funded. A slush fund of hundreds of thousands of dollars was maintained by CRP to pay people to bug the offices and infiltrate the campaigns of Democratic candidates to get information and sabotage their campaign efforts.

Bernstein learned about the activities of lawyer Donald Segretti through a call from someone who had heard about Segretti's attempts to recruit people for the dirty-tricks campaign. The story was confirmed by a man Segretti had tried to hire as well as by other sources. This man gave an example of one way Segretti's people would sabotage a candidate. Pretending to be campaign workers, they would call a convention hall and reschedule a speech to a later time so that the building would be locked when the candidate arrived.

The most famous dirty trick was the "Canuck Letter" that destroyed the campaign of Edmund Muskie, the strongest Democratic contender. The letter had claimed that Muskie supported using the derogatory term "Canucks" for French Canadians. It turned out that the deputy director of communications in the White House had written that letter. The dirty-tricks campaign, one Justice Department attorney told Bernstein, was "basic strategy that goes all the way to the top."

Woodward and Bernstein knew that the real issue was who had planned the dirty-tricks campaign and Watergate. But the reporters had little hard information connecting the White House to the events. The *Post* was risking its reputation by trusting the instincts and anonymous sources of its two young reporters.

Now, however, many national newspapers and magazines were following the case. As the election neared, the White House turned from vague denials to accusations that Democratic rival George McGovern's campaign was working with the *Post* to smear the Nixon White House.

But Woodward and Bernstein were getting closer to the truth. They learned that the president's personal lawyer and the deputy assistant to the president had authorized payments from the CRP fund to political saboteurs. Now it was clear that White House officials were involved with political spying and sabotage.

South Dakota senator George McGovern was widely seen as the weakest Democratic contender against Nixon. Since the Republicans' "dirty-tricks" campaign had helped to damage the other candidates, McGovern won the Democratic nomination.

On October 24, 1972, two weeks before Election Day, the reporters ran a story claiming that Hugh Sloan's grand-jury testimony had identified H. R. Haldeman, assistant to the president and White House chief of staff, as one of the people in control of the secret CRP fund. Publishing this article was a terrible mistake. Although the reporters had been unable to convince any source to state directly that Haldeman had ordered payments to be made from the fund, four sources—Deep Throat, an FBI agent, a Justice Department attorney, and Sloan himself—had not warned them off the story when Woodward and Bernstein outlined it to them. But the reporters had made a bad assumption. Sloan had not stated Haldeman's connection in grand-jury testimony. Because of this error,

Sloan's lawyer and the White House were able to deny the story outright. The *Post*'s credibility seemed to be shot.

On top of this setback, President Richard Nixon was reelected by a landslide on November 7, winning almost 62 percent of the popular vote and 97 percent of the electoral vote. Two months later, five of the seven men arrested in connection with the Watergate burglary pleaded guilty. The other two—Liddy and McCord—went to trial and were both found guilty. Having concluded that the Watergate break-in conspiracy was limited to the seven indicted men, prosecutors from the Justice Department asked no questions about who authorized CRP payments to the burglars.

In his trial, G. Gordon Liddy was made the Watergate "fall guy." Justice Department prosecutors contended that he had planned and carried out the Watergate operation without authorization.

Then the White House's luck began to run out. After several months of closed-door hearings, the U.S. Senate began nationally televised hearings investigating the Watergate incident in May 1973. Information leading to the resignations or firings of the president's top men— White House Counsel John W. Dean III, White House Chief of Staff H. R. Haldeman, and Assistant to the President for Domestic Affairs John D. Ehrlichman— had come out in the closed-door testimony. Still, Richard Nixon repeatedly stated that he had known nothing about plans for the burglary or the cover-up.

As the hearings continued that summer, John Dean testified before the Watergate Committee that President Nixon had been aware of the Watergate burglary and had also approved the cover-up. An aide testified that Nixon had tape-recorded secret meetings discussing Watergate. When the committee subpoenaed the taped recordings of conversations about Watergate, Nixon refused to provide them. He said that as president he had an executive privilege to ignore the subpoena.

Under intense public pressure, Nixon did finally turn over the subpoenaed tapes in October, but over 18 minutes of material was missing from one tape. This gap convinced many Americans that Nixon had been lying about his innocence. Additional information about political favors to businesses that donated large sums to CRP, evidence of other burglaries and espionage, and the revelation that the White House employed a group dubbed the "Plumbers" to stop leaks to the press eventually sealed the fate of President Richard M. Nixon.

In July 1974, more than one year after the hearings began, the Judiciary Committee of the United States House of Representatives voted to impeach the president because of his involvement in the scandal and his obstruction of justice. On August 9, before he could be impeached, Nixon resigned from office.

When Richard Nixon boarded the helicopter after his resignation, he signed the "V" for victory, as if he were leaving in triumph, not disgrace.

Woodward and Bernstein won the coveted Pulitzer Prize for their series of articles on Watergate, which had helped lead to the Senate investigation and Nixon's resignation. The two reporters received further accolades when their book about their investigation of the Watergate scandal, *All the President's Men*, was published on June 17, 1974—the second anniversary of the Watergate break-in. The book became a national bestseller, selling more than 4 million copies.

In 1976, *All the President's Men* was made into a motion picture with Hollywood stars Robert Redford and Dustin Hoffman playing Woodward and Bernstein

Robert Redford, playing Woodward, watches Dustin Hoffman's Bernstein type a story in the Washington Post *office in the movie version of* All the President's Men.

respectively. The image of journalists as heroes seeking truth and fighting corruption inspired many people to study journalism.

Woodward and Bernstein published *The Final Days*, an account of the end of Nixon's tenure as president, in 1976. Each of the reporters had made hundreds of thousands of dollars from their two books and the movie. They would never have to worry about money again, but fame and fortune brought them problems as well.

While Woodward remained at the *Post*, Bernstein left the paper in 1976 and began writing magazine articles. In 1979, the ABC television network, seeking someone with star quality to attract viewers, named Bernstein its Washington bureau chief. Although Bernstein had been reporting for almost 20 years, he had never worked in television news. The arrogant reporter was not a good hire and was not qualified to supervise the seasoned television journalists at the station. In 1981, ABC finally demoted him to a regular news correspondent.

The same year Bernstein was hired by ABC, Woodward was promoted to assistant managing editor of the metropolitan section of the *Post*. Not long after his promotion, one of the most embarrassing scandals in the *Post*'s history occurred. In September 1980, Janet Cooke, a newly hired *Post* reporter, wrote "Jimmy's World," a lengthy article about an eight-year-old heroin addict. The story was a sensation and was picked up by 300 other newspapers and *U.S. News & World Report*.

Cooke's piece so impressed Woodward that he recommended that the *Post* nominate "Jimmy's World" for a

Pulitzer Prize. Like Woodward and Bernstein before her, Janet Cooke won the most prestigious prize in journalism for her series.

But then the *Post* began receiving telephone calls from several of Cooke's former colleagues. Cooke had lied about her credentials to get her job. Under intense questioning by Woodward and other editors, she also confessed that she had never interviewed an eight-year-old heroin addict. When she wrote the story, Cooke had told her editors she had 145 pages of notes to back up her reporting, but "Jimmy's World" was completely made up. Shamefaced, the *Post* revealed the story's inaccuracy and returned the Pulitzer Prize.

The Cooke scandal wore on Woodward, and his reporters complained that he was too edgy and indecisive to be an effective leader. A few months after Cooke left the paper, the *Post* asked Woodward to go back to being an investigative reporter for the paper.

Woodward continued to have success as a writer, however. His often controversial books include: *Wired: The Short Life and Fast Times of John Belushi*; *The Brethren: Inside the Supreme Court*; *Veil: The Secret Wars of the CIA*; *The Commanders* (about George Bush's presidential administration); *The Man Who Would Be President: Dan Quayle* (written with fellow *Post* reporter David Broder); *The Agenda: Inside the Clinton White House*; and *The Choice* (which examined the 1996 presidential campaign). In September 1997, Woodward broke a story for the *Post* about Vice-President Al Gore making illegal fundraising calls from his White House office.

Bernstein, too, continued to write. In 1989, his book *Loyalties: A Son's Memoir* was published. The book explored growing up with Communist parents in the years of Senator Joseph McCarthy's anti-Communist witch-hunt. Communism was also a theme of his 1996 book, *His Holiness: John Paul II and the Hidden History of Our Time*, in which Bernstein and coauthor Marco Politi examined the role of the U.S. government and the Vatican in the fall of Communism. Over the years, Bernstein has also written articles for *Time* and other magazines.

During the past 25 years, the term "Watergate" has come to stand for all types of conspiracy or corruption in the White House. Every major controversy involving a presidential administration acquires the suffix "-gate." For example, during the early 1990s reporters frequently referred to a controversial real-estate venture involving President Bill Clinton as "Whitewatergate." A scandal involving firings in the White House travel office during the Clinton administration was dubbed "travelgate."

The post-Watergate public will not forget the potential for corruption among high-ranking officials. Many journalists consider their function as "watchdog" of the government to be the most important role of the press.

Bibliography

Bernstein, Carl, and Bob Woodward. *All the President's Men*. New York: Simon & Schuster, 1974.

Careless, J. M. S. *Brown of the* Globe: *The Voice of Upper Canada*. 2 vols. Toronto: Macmillan, 1959.

Chaney, Lindsay, and Michael Cieply. *The Hearsts: Family and Empire—The Later Years*. New York: Simon & Schuster, 1981.

Dicken-Garcia, Hazel. *Journalistic Standards in Nineteenth-Century America*. Madison: University of Wisconsin Press, 1989.

Dillon, Merton L. *Elijah P. Lovejoy: Abolitionist Editor*. Urbana: University of Illinois Press, 1961.

Emery, Edwin, and Michael Emery. *The Press and America: An Interpretive History of the Mass Media*. Englewood Cliffs, N.J.: Prentice Hall, 1988.

Fang, Irving E. *Those Radio Commentators*. Ames: Iowa State University Press, 1977.

Ferris, Paul. *The House of Northcliffe: A Biography of an Empire*. New York: World Publishing, 1972.

Fleming, Thomas. *The Story of American Newspapers: Behind the Headlines*. New York: Walker, 1989.

Frazier, Nancy. *William Randolph Hearst: Press Baron*. Englewood Cliffs, N.J.: Silver Burdett Press, 1989.

Greeley, Horace. *Recollections of a Busy Life*. New York: J. B. Ford, 1968.

Grey, Elizabeth. *The Story of Journalism*. Boston: Houghton Mifflin, 1969.

Griffiths, Dennis, ed. *The Encyclopedia of the British Press, 1422-1992*. New York: St. Martin's Press, 1992.

Havill, Adrian. *Deep Truth: The Lives of Bob Woodward and Carl Bernstein*. New York: Birch Lane Press, 1993.

Higham, Charles. *The Films of Orson Welles*. Los Angeles: University of California Press, 1970.

Homer, Harlan Hoyt. *Lincoln and Greeley*. Urbana: University of Illinois Press, 1953.

Kochersberger, Robert C., Jr., ed. *More Than a Muckraker: Ida Tarbell's Lifetime in Journalism*. Knoxville: University of Tennessee Press, 1994.

Leonard, Thomas C. *The Power of the Press: The Birth of American Political Reporting*. New York: Oxford University Press, 1986.

Lewis, John. *George Brown*. Toronto: Morang, 1907.

Lunde, Erik S. *Horace Greeley*. Boston: Twayne, 1981.

Murrow, Edward R. *In Search of Light: The Broadcasts of Edward R. Murrow, 1938-1961*. New York: Knopf, 1967.

Paneth, Donald. *The Encyclopedia of American Journalism*. New York: Facts on File, 1983.

Rawson, Hugh. "The Words of Watergate." *American Heritage*, October 1997.

Regier, C. C. *The Era of the Muckrakers*. Gloucester, Mass.: Peter Smith, 1957.

Ryan, A. P. *Lord Northcliffe*. London: Collins, 1953.

Schudson, Michael. *Watergate in American Memory: How We Remember, Forget, and Reconstruct the Past.* New York: Basic Books, 1993.

Simon, Paul. *Freedom's Champion—Elijah Lovejoy.* Carbondale: Southern Illinois University Press, 1994.

Sloan, David, and Julie Hedgepeth Williams. *The Early American Press, 1690-1783.* Westport, Conn.: Greenwood Press, 1994.

Sperber, Ann M. *Murrow: His Life and Times.* New York: Freundlich Books, 1986.

Swanberg, W. A. *Citizen Hearst: A Biography of William Randolph Hearst.* New York: Scribner's, 1961.

Taylor, S. J. *The Great Outsiders: Northcliffe, Rothermere and the* Daily Mail. London: Weidenfeld and Nicolson, 1996.

Index

154

ABOUT THE AUTHOR

JAMES SATTER is a book editor and former magazine writer who lives in Minneapolis. He has a bachelor's degree in journalism from the University of Minnesota and is pursuing a master's degree in the history of science and technology. This is his first book.

Photo Credits
Photographs courtesy of: p. 6, *St. Paul Daily News*, Minnesota Historical Society; pp. 9, 10, 16, 19, 21, 22, 27, 28, 30, 33, 34, 36, 37, 44, 51, 64, 67, 69, 73, 75, 79, 82, 84, 85, 89, 93, 98, 109, 112, 119, 120, 123, Library of Congress; pp. 12, 43, 77, 91, 126, Minnesota Historical Society; p. 13, Paul Almasy/ ©Mike Corrado Corbis; pp. 14, 103, *Famous Nineteenth Century Faces*, Art Direction Book Co.; p. 39, The Library of Virginia; p. 41, *Harper's Weekly* (Jan. 24, 1863), Minnesota Historical Society; p. 42, *Harper's Weekly* (Nov. 16, 1867), Minnesota Historical Society; pp. 46, 49, 54, 56, 61, National Archives of Canada; p. 59, Western Canada Pictorial Index; pp. 76, 104, 135, 136, 138, 142, 143, 145, National Archives; p. 81, Manuscripts Department, Lilly Library, Indiana University, Bloomington, IN; p. 96, League of Women Voters; p. 110, Seely G. Mudd Manuscript Library, Princeton University Libraries; p. 117, Archives of the Simon Wiesenthal Center; p. 127, O. J. Rapp, LBJ Library Collection; p. 128, Archive Photos / Jim Wells; pp. 131, 133, Marylandia Collection, University of Maryland; p. 146, Archive Photos.